INSTANT EXPERT

W9-BGM-166

COLLECTING
ART DECO

Tony Fusco

HOUSE OF COLLECTIBLES
NEW YORK

First Edition

0 9 8 7 6 5 4 3 2 1

May 2004

ISBN: 0-375-72042-1

> A
, 709.0349

CONTENTS

For our friend, Jacques Caussin, in recognition of all that he has done to promote an appreciation of Art Deco and 20th century design over the past three decades.

ACKNOWLEDGMENTS

The world of Art Deco is so vast, a project like this would not be possible without the help of an army of "experts." I would like to personally thank the following individuals for their help, many of whom I have worked with over the years: Robert Aibel, Moderne, PA; Caroline Birenbaum, Swann Galleries, NY; Gary and Janet Calderwood, Calderwood Gallery, PA; Ric Emmett, Modernism Gallery, FL; Lorial and Bryan Francis, DecoDame.com, FL; Denis Gallion and Daniel Morris, Historical Design Collection, NY; Eric Menard and Peter Linden, Decodence, CA; Jane Prentiss, Skinner, Inc., Boston, and many other colleagues new and old who contributed photos. Special thanks to Elissa Swanger at Phillips, de Pury & Luxembourg; my assistant Amy Lavoie for her work on the Resource Guide; and my longtime friend and editor Dottie Harris for her persistence and patience. Most of all, I thank my partner Robert Four for his outstanding photography and his unfailing support of my "Decomania."

Grateful acknowledgment is also made to the following for use of their photographs on the front cover of this book:

Top row:

Aluminum and frosted glass table Pattyn Lamp, Modern Products Corporation, ca. 1935. Courtesy of Decodence, CA

Lounge chair with brushed polished chrome, wood, and leather upholstery by Gilbert Rohde, ca. 1934. Courtesy of Historical Design Collection, NY.

Mantel clock in carved gilded wood by Georges de Bardyere, French, ca. 1925. Courtesy of Calderwood Gallery, PA.

Vintage photo of actress Jean Harlow in an Art Deco photo frame. Courtesy of Steve Starr Studios, IL.

Bottom row:

Three-panel screen by Donald Deskey, ca. 1929. Courtesy of Modernism Gallery, FL.

Susie Cooper, "Kestrel," demitasse set, ca. 1930. Author file photo. Courtesy of Linda Cheverton.

Fada Radio Model L-56, 1939, made of catalin plastic. Author file photo. Courtesy of John Sideli.

Chair by Sue et Mare, French, 1920, for the ocean liner *Paris*. Courtesy of Calderwood Gallery, PA.

INTRODUCTION: BECOMING AN ART DECO EXPERT

The only thing you really need to know to be considered an Art Deco expert is how to identify what is—and what is not—Art Deco. It sounds simple but, unfortunately, it's something on which not all Art Deco experts seem to fully agree.

The term "Art Deco" itself only came into popular usage during the late 1960s, and is derived from the title of the 1925 Parisian Exposition Internationale des Arts Décoratifs et Industriels Modernes, which emphasized the "Arts Décoratifs" or the decorative arts: furniture, glass, ceramics, textiles, and the like.

Wrongly thought by many to be the starting point of the Art Deco style, the 1925 Exposition actually marked the culmination of a *de luxe* French Art Deco and the emergence of a more geometric, Germanic-influenced "Modern" style.

Today, accurately or not, the term "Art Deco" is applied to a whole complex of trends in the decorative and applied arts, architecture, and the fine arts in the period roughly between 1909 and 1939. I say "roughly" because there are earlier designs that strongly foreshadow the Art Deco style, and elements of the style lingered well into the 1940s and 1950s.

Among the many early influences that contributed to the emergence of the Art Deco style were the opulent sets and costumes of Les Ballets Russes which arrived in Paris in 1909 and set off an explosion in the design and fashion world. However, the full development of the style was delayed by the advent of World War I. A few years thereafter, French interior designers, fine furniture makers, and the boutique workshops of the great Parisian department stores took the spotlight at the 1925 Exposition.

For the most part, these early French designers worked with expensive woods and exotic materials for a wealthy clientele, who commissioned them to produce handmade, often unique items. Even the design boutiques within the Parisian department stores commissioned household decorations and furnishings in relatively small series. These early French designers would be horrified to learn today that their work is identified by the same name as that of the Moderns who thought of furniture as "household equipment," introducing such items as chairs made with tubular steel. Even further removed from luxurious French Art Deco were the broadly mass-produced furniture, appliances, chrome, and ceramics of the Depression-era 1930s in America.

The emergence of the Bauhaus as an important school of design in Germany in the late 1920s and early 1930s strongly affected French and American designers after 1925. It was this Modern style that became popular in America, due in part to the ease with which objects could be fashioned for industrial mass production. This popularity was also due, no doubt, to the large number of talented designers from Austria, Germany, and Scandinavian countries who emigrated to the U.S. In America, the icons of this "phase" of the Art Deco style are undoubtedly the skyscraper and the zigzag imagery evoked by Jazz.

What one could call the last "phase" of the Art Deco style fully reflected the impact of the "industrial designer" on transportation, machines, and household appliances in the 1930s, and is referred to by many as "Streamline." Reflected in the sleek, smooth, bullet-nosed designs for the railway "Streamliners," the style was soon applied to everything from ceramic dinnerware, to toasters and lawn mowers.

Perhaps this complex evolution is why there is such confusion when someone uses the term "Art Deco." Adding to the confusion is the fact that as Art Deco spread to become the first truly international design style. It was confronted and changed dramatically by national preferences, cultural differences, social, and economic forces.

In addition, scholars have traced many of the influences on Art Deco to turn-of-the-century and pre–World War I design movements: Art Nouveau, Arts and Crafts, the Vienna Secession, the Glasgow School in Scotland, Cubism, the De Stijl movement in Holland, and Italian Futurism. All too often people wrongly refer to these design movements as Art Deco. In today's marketplace, you'll still hear people incorrectly refer to a 1940s "Biomorphic" chair or a 1950s boomerang-style coffee table as Art Deco.

Not only was Art Deco influenced by European design movements, it was also highly influenced by the design of numerous traditional and ancient cultures: Egyptian, Japanese, sub-Saharan Africa, Mayan and Aztec cultures, and others. Some popular "Art Deco" designs are direct copies of motifs from these ancient civilizations!

Dozens of other names have been coined in an attempt to come up with something better, or to name a specific style within the style: Twenties Decorative, Jazz Modern, Style Moderne, Depression Modern, International Style, American Modern, Machine Age, Zigzag, and others have all been used. Early French designers did not call their style "Art Deco," but some referred to it as Poiret Style, because of the highly influential designer Paul Poiret. New designations are frequently used to imply a regional style, such as Florida's "Tropical Deco," and the Native American–influenced "Pueblo Deco" of the Southwest. In a spirit of fun, the restrained Art Deco public buildings, post offices and courthouses that sprang up under the Works Progress Administration (WPA) are sometimes called "Greco Deco."

In America, Art Deco also became highly associated with Hollywood. The costumes, set designs, furnishings for movies, posters, and other Hollywood design from the 1920s through the 1940s helped to popularize the style to the widest possible audience. In the end, perhaps, it was Hollywood's "Screen Deco"—a continual exaggeration of the style—that caused Art Deco to fall out of favor with designers. No leading-edge designer wants to be thought of as merely repeating what is already popular.

Many think a final, great explosion of Art Deco design came with the New York World's Fair of 1939. This was soon followed by the real explosion of World War II, the final blow to a style thought of as just "too chic," and "too cheeky" for wartime.

How far Art Deco had metamorphosed from the extremely delicate eggshell lacquer of Jean Dunand, the exceptional glass sculptures of René Lalique, and the sharkskin-covered exotic furniture of Jacques-Émile Ruhlmann to the mass-produced household furnishings of the Depression, streamlined automobiles, and the razzmatazz of Hollywood!

Throughout this book, we'll try to show examples of how Art Deco evolved through each of its three major design "phases"—French Art Deco, Modern, and Streamline—to help you better recognize, understand, and appreciate it.

1

FROM ARTISTE DÉCORATEUR TO INDUSTRIAL DESIGNER

Design in a World of Change

Before World War I, urbanites "with taste" in the United States and France were reading by the light of their Tiffany lamps, which epitomized the Art Nouveau style, and modeling their ideals of feminine beauty on Alphonse Mucha's curvaceous females with tendril-like hair.

Art Nouveau was dominant for a relatively short period of time, and was not as widespread as one might believe, given its popularity today. Most urban Americans, for example, were still living in modest, post-Victorian or neo-Colonial settings, still immune to the lures of the advertising poster and shocked by the seductive goddesses of Art Nouveau.

In England and America, the moralistic Arts and Crafts movement looked down on the extravagance of Art Nouveau. In addition, in several other European countries, emerging modernist design movements reacted against the flowery decoration and over-ornamentation of the Art Nouveau style.

Just after the turn of the century, early pioneers of new modern styles included architects Joseph Maria Olbrich and Josef Hoffmann in Vienna, who created angular silver tea sets and restrained bentwood furniture; the Scottish architect and designer Charles Rennie Mackintosh; and German architects Otto Wagner and Adolf Loos, who influenced the De Stijl group of Holland and later the German Bauhaus.

These designers would initially not have as much impact on design in France as did the arrival in Paris in 1909 of Diaghilev's Les Ballets Russes. Many talented young fashion designers and artists were captivated by the colorful costumes and Oriental influence of its set and costume designs.

Among those most influenced by Les Ballets Russes were such notable fashion designers, interior designers, and illustrators as Paul Poiret, Paul Iribe, Paul Follot, Erté, Georges Lepape, and André Marty.

Many fashion designers moved into the field of interior design, becoming interior designers, or *ensembliers* (literally, someone who creates an "ensemble"), for wealthy Parisian clients. Poiret's firm Martine sought to entirely integrate the "look" of a room, and therefore commissioned or created its own textiles, pottery, porcelain, and wallpaper, as well as furniture. A room became the vision of one designer, rather than a collection of the works of many. Poiret made no bones about the fact that he wanted to control every aspect of design in a client's home, right down to the throw pillows on the low-slung divan.

Jacques Doucet, an important fashion designer, was very influential and was considered *avant-garde*, a military term that roughly translates as "leading edge." He collected Cubist paintings, early Surrealist works, and exotic African and Chinese art.

He commissioned and bought from talented designers to furnish his own home: Pierre Legrain, Clément Rousseau, Eileen Gray, Gustav Miklos, and René Lalique. It is said that André Breton, the fiery father of Surrealism, helped Doucet select his contemporary art.

Doucet had great influence with the younger generation of designers, as well. Paul Poiret was a former employee of Doucet's when his career was at its highest. Poiret, in turn, would hire notable designers such as Paul Iribe and Georges Barbier to execute or render illustrations of his designs. Poiret traveled to Vienna and Moscow, where he met a young man named Romain de Tirtoff, who simplifed his name to Erté, based on the French pronunciation of his initials, R. T.

Many of the best furniture designers were working to combine exotic or new materials, traditional methods, and simpler design. These *ébénistes*, or "cabinetmakers," also worked for wealthy, knowledgeable, and status-conscious clients. The word "*ébéniste*" derives from ebony, the expensive, imported wood that was often used to craft furniture.

After the World War I, architect Louis Süe and painter-decorator André Mare founded the Compagnie des Arts Français. They were among the first to bring together artists from many disciplines in their search for "total design." Their company designed and commissioned ceramics, glassware, bookbindings, textiles, and furniture, as well as architecture.

Süe et Mare were among those designers who considered themselves "tastefully modern," as did many of their talented contemporaries such as Jacques-Émile Ruhlmann who had his first major exhibition at the Salon d'Automne in 1913. Other designers of this period include Maurice Dufrène, Jean Dunand, Léon Jallot, Edgar Brandt, Raoul Dufy, and Jules Leleu. The production of designers such as these dominated French decorative arts until 1925. In fact, it was their overwhelming strength and influence in the right circles that kept more Modernist designs from appearing in the 1925 Exposition.

Many people wrongly believe that Art Deco was a revolt against Art Nouveau as the dominant style. French Art Deco was not a "movement"—it had no name at the time, no books had been written to establish the "rules" of the new design style, and no angry theorists argued for the adoption of Art Deco over Art Nouveau. While these artists did seek to find new, more simplified lines, forms, and stylized decorations, they were really part of a continuum of French traditional design and often looked back at French 18th-century furniture for inspiration. Even when the more Modern style became prevalent, the grand style of the early Art Deco designers would prevail in official commissions for ocean liners and public buildings into the 1930s.

If a center for the new design was to be identified, it would perhaps be the Société des Artistes Décorateurs, founded in 1900, to which many of the designers named above belonged.

An "*artiste décorateur*," as the name implies, considered him- or herself an "artist" as well as a "decorator" who produced furnishings and objects, or "decorative arts." The new design ideas of these decorative artists were spread by the society's annual "salons" or exhibitions featuring their latest creations, and by magazines such as *Art et Décoration* and *L'Art Décoratif*.

The new style was popularized through French department stores, which carried high-quality furniture and decorative objects such as Lalique glass and Longwy pottery. Each major French department store had its own *atelier*, or "workshop," to create exclusive designs. These specialized boutiques were headed by some of the best designers of the day, and gave commissions to still others. Their contributions to early French Art Deco design were apparent at their pavilions for the 1925 Paris Exposition.

However, even as this luxurious Art Deco style evolved and gained a wider acceptance in the Parisian upper-middle class, it faced pressure from the modern design movements in other countries and from the changes that were taking place in society.

Early modernist designers in France maintained a hand-crafted aesthetic, but were less resistant to the use of machines, new techniques, and modern, less-expensive materials. One notable event that impacted early French modern designers was the 1910 exhibition of the Deutscher Werkbund in Paris. This early German work-shop and its machine-made design influenced such French designers as Francis Jourdain, René Herbst, René Joubert, Robert Mallet-Stevens, and Le Corbusier.

Décoration Interieur Moderne, or DIM, founded in 1919 under the direction of René Joubert, was the first French firm to create tubular steel furniture starting in about 1922. The ideals and designs of these modern artists would not gain wide acceptance until after 1925, when the *de luxe* phase of Art Deco was no longer a reality in economic and social terms, and when influences from other countries were clamoring too loudly to be ignored.

After 1925, the Modern movement gained strongholds across Europe. The centers of the movement were the German Bauhaus school and the Parisian Union des Artistes Modernes, founded by those who did not gain acceptance into the Salon des Artistes Décorateurs, which had now become the "design establishment."

By 1928, the company Thonet was producing tubular bent steel furniture designed by Le Corbusier. In 1931 Practical Equipment Limited, or PEL, was creating mod-ern metal furniture for a wealthy clientele in England. By the mid-1930s, even Süe et Mare were making alu-minum furniture in a Modern style.

The "Machine Age" was coming into maturity, and inter-national travel and the exchange of ideas was facilitated by "the wireless," telephones, the passenger train, steamships and airplanes. The stock market crash of 1929, and the ensuing worldwide Depression became the social and economic imperative for mass-produced furnishings made from less expensive materials.

The Modern movement clearly broke with the past, ded-icated itself to the use of new materials, and adopted a socialistic view of their role in society. Unlike the early

French Art Deco style, Modernism did have its doctrines and manifestos, which overtly proclaimed it to be an attempt to bring together art and industry. Its primary goal was to create less expensive, yet still well-designed, furnishings and other objects. Its optimistic political goal was to put the machine to the service of the masses.

In America, groundbreaking modern designers had been at work since the run of the century. Frank Lloyd Wright, influenced by Louis Sullivan and by the Arts and Crafts Movement, had been creating modern architectural designs since around 1900. Joseph Urban, a member of the Vienna Secession, emigrated to America and founded the Wiener Werkstätte, or "Vienna Workshops," gallery in New York in 1922. Paul Theodore Frankl was building his "skyscraper" bookcases as early as 1925.

Although Art Deco and Modern were set in opposition to each another, both put an emphasis on quality styling, even though handcrafting slowly gave way to mass production. One way of describing the transition that took place is that Art Deco design first reflected the handcrafted French luxury of the *artiste décorateur*, and later the German and American economically influenced functionalism of a machine aesthetic.

In the United States, French Art Deco did not gain wide acceptance. In fact, a number of manufacturers from the U.S. had visited the 1925 Paris Exposition, but came away unimpressed. In 1926 a collection of objects from the 1925 Paris Exposition traveled to New York, Boston, Philadelphia, Detroit, and other cities. Department stores such as Macy's and Lord & Taylor in New York, Barker Brothers in Los Angeles, and Gimbel's in Pittsburgh hosted special showings of Parisian design.

However the French style of Art Deco continued to be seen essentially as a "foreign" style, although it did greatly influence Hollywood through designers such as Erté, who came to America in 1925 and began designing sets and costumes for the screen almost immediately.

Designers from Scandinavia, Germany and Austria would have a wider impact than the French in this country. Finnish architect/designer Eliel Saarinen became the first director of the Cranbrook Academy of Art, near Detroit, in 1922. American ceramic artists from Ohio exchanged visits with artists from Vienna. Architects Walter Gropius and Marcel Breuer would establish themselves in this country to avoid the rise of fascism in Germany.

The Modern style fit America's rapid industrialization, and quickly captured the entire market. It created a staggering variety of both functional and decorative high- and low-cost objects during the 1920s and 1930s, which are sought after by Art Deco collectors today.

It was clear that the new Modernism was the major design style of the day as early as the 1929 exhibition. "The Architect and the Industrial Arts," at the Metropolitan Museum of Art in New York, which highlighted rooms of furnishings designed by architects. Design for the machine's rise to the status of art was confirmed in 1934 by both the "Contemporary American Industrial Art" exhibition at the Metropolitan Museum of Art and the "Machine Art" exhibition at New York's Museum of Modern Art.

As production increased, manufacturers began to rely increasingly on industrial designers to style products both to public tastes and to mass-production. In many cases, the leading industrial designers, such as Norman Bel Geddes, came from the world of advertising or the theater.

Bel Geddes was a New York City theater set designer, and worked for one of America's first major advertising agencies, J. Walter Thompson. Bel Geddes coined the term "industrial designer" in 1927, at the age of thirty-three, when he opened the first industrial design studio. By the 1930s the term had become widely accepted, although other terms such as "design engineer," "consumer engineer," and "product designer," were also used.

In 1929 Bel Geddes was hired as design consultant for the upcoming 1933 Chicago "Century of Progress" Exposition. His book *Horizons*, published in 1932, promoted his theories of industrial art. He felt that the same emotional response one has when viewing great works of art like the Parthenon or the paintings of Michelangelo should be felt in response to everyday objects. He designed everything from gas stoves to the interior of Pan American Airways clipper airplanes. He went on to design the General Motors Pavilion, "City of Tomorrow" for the 1939 World's Fair.

The economic revolution of personal credit came into existence at this time. The advent of credit had the advantage of opening up huge new markets for manufacturers. Another new animal, the annual model change, began to appear. Model changes were, and still are, meant to increase consumption by casting older models as "out of style." Wider varieties of sizes and colors were introduced, as well as broader lines of consumer items.

To spur consumption, manufacturers turned to talented graphic designers and advertising illustrators to render products on paper and in many cases, to design the products themselves. This was especially imperative after the stock market crash of 1929 and during the Depression that followed.

The result of the crash and Depression was a re-design and advertising frenzy. From the late 1920s through the 1930s, leading American architects and industrial designers such as Walter Dorwin Teague, Raymond Loewy, Donald Deskey, Kem Weber, Gilbert Rohde, Walter von Nessen, Russel Wright and others were commissioned to design and redesign furniture and other articles for mass production: glass, chrome, appliances, radios, lamps, and office equipment.

The 1934 Industrial Arts Exposition, held at Rockefeller Center in New York, displayed such industrial designs as a Todd "protectograph," designed by Henry Dreyfuss, a Coca-Cola dispenser designed by John Vassos, a Quiet May oil burner designed by Donald Deskey, and a refrigerator designed by Lurelle Guild for the Norge Corporation.

Walter Dorwin Teague designed glassware for Steuben Glass, tabletop and floor model radios, the Kodak Bantam Special and other cameras, and desk lamps for the Polaroid Corporation. He conceived Con Edison's "City of Light" and the giant National Cash Register at the 1939 New York World's Fair.

Teague was also a leading theorist for Industrial Design. As he wrote in an article entitled "Designing for Machines" in the April 2, 1930 issue of *Advertising Arts* magazine:

"Like it or not, we find ourselves living in a Machine Age, an Age of Power, an Age of Mass Production. Here is the greatest problem of design: to adapt itself to machine and mass production. Our job is to make the machines bring forth beauty….And don't tell anybody that this is Modern Art: keep that as a secret among ourselves. By the time this age realizes what Modern Art really means, we shall be living in a frame of beauty, heartily and gustily enjoying it, rich in the possession of authentic style, happy once more in a harmonious, coordinated environment where we feel luxuriously at home."

The complete fulfillment of this vision was not to be. A friend of mine says he was totally disillusioned as a child when the fabulous things he saw at the New York World's Fair of 1939 never came to pass, and World War II seemed to erase the 1930s vision of "Progress via the Machine." Today, some industrial designers' concepts for how the future would look read like science fiction.

Though the outstanding industrial designs of the period do capture and embody the spirit in which they were produced, in many mass-produced items, cheaper materials only underscored poor design. This type of production has created a lasting bad impression of what Art Deco really means. Poor chromium plating, base metals painted to appear as bronze, dime-store ceramic statues are evidence that the style was in decline. Although some of these have become "Art Deco icons" in the collecting world today and fetch high prices, they were dismissed as "kitsch," a German word meaning "trash".

Earlier in the Art Deco movement, even when the object was made in quantity, it was still a controlled production. At that time, the French term *article de séries* indicated simply that an object was not unique. Today the term is used derisively, for even French-made goods have succumbed to the need to produce cheap, manufactured household items for the millions of people who inhabit urban centers.

High style adapted to industrial production meant that the masses could enjoy at least the illusion of grandeur that had been the standard of Art Deco design. However, the trend toward poorly manufactured goods would increase as the Depression wore on. Hollywood movies were the best escape from troubled times, and "having style" was a way of pretending times weren't so bad. Hollywood producers engaged the talents of designers such as Kem Weber, Joseph Urban, Coco Chanel, Hermès, and the styles on the screen became yearned for by the masses. Hollywood borrowed and glamorized the Art Deco style, and in the process "standardized" it for mass consumption.

The proliferation of Modern and Streamline memorabilia that accompanied the New York World's Fair of 1939, on the brink of World War II, was the style's "last hurrah." More than fifty million people streamed through "the future." When that future did not come to pass, and a terrible war took place instead, it's no wonder that Americans turned their back on the style.

One of the secrets of having "style" and "taste," however, is that it belongs to an "in" crowd. It seems that the moment a design trend or style becomes truly popular, it begins to decline, even if Art Deco had survived the war, it would not have survived popularization. Designers and artists, always looking for new ground, had begun to turn away from the style long before the public did.

Today, the Art Deco collecting field runs the gamut from luxurious pieces designed by the French *artistes décorateurs* to the mass-produced output of American industrial designers in the 1930s.

The transition of the style is evident in every area: from a fine macassar ebony desk by Ruhlmann, to the inventive tubular chrome "Z" stool by Gilbert Rohde; from a rare eggshell lacquer bookbinding to 1930s geometric paper dust jackets for books; from a silver coffee set with quartz handles by Jean Puiforcat to Walter von Nessen's streamlined cocktail shaker designs for Chase Chrome; from the exquisite jewelry of Cartier to jazzy Bakelite plastic bracelets; from hand-painted studio ceramics to bold-colored "Refrigerator Ware" from Hall China; from a rare sapphire blue vase by Lalique to Anchor Hocking's stylish "Manhattan" Depression glass.

One of the joys of being a collector of Art Deco is that no matter where you stand along this continuum, no matter what you collect, you can see into the past and catch a glimpse of the once-possible future. Through the evolution of Art Deco design, you can witness how the world was changing. ◾

2

RECOGNIZING ART DECO

Motifs

Knowing the design motifs that were used in Art Deco can help you recognize it, and also help distinguish it from other styles, such as Art Nouveau. In each phase of Art Deco, a number of design motifs were created, seized upon by designers setting the trends, extensively using the design "vocabulary" of the day, and then were forsaken as their overuse made them "old hat."

Art Nouveau Motifs

The Art Nouveau style was characterized by curving, swaying lines in asymmetrical patterns. Plant imagery was used frequently: tendril-like vines such as morning glories, entwined leaves, and flowers such as calla lilies.

Typical figures were women with flowing hair who were more full-bodied than the later, sleeker Art Deco female figures. The mermaid was a popular Art Nouveau motif, and animal motifs included snakes, dragonflies, peacocks, and lizards. Toward the end of the period, many designers felt that Art Nouveau ornamentation had become excessive and sought a new design vocabulary that would respond to a more modern sensibility.

The "frozen fountain motif in a glazed terra cotta architectural detail, ca. 1925. Author's collection. Photo by Robert Four.

Early French Art Deco Motifs

Although emphasizing a simplicity of line and form, early French Art Deco designers used still somewhat romantic, though more highly stylized, motifs: bubbles, rainbows, and flowing water. Flowers and ferns were still used, but their lines were simplified and the overall effect was that of a symmetrical pattern. One frequently sees stylized baskets and cornucopias of fruits and flowers on everything from clocks to compacts. The "frozen fountain" was a particularly popular motif, used frequently in both furnishings and architecture.

Lithe women without the flowing robes and hairstyles of the Art Nouveau period became popular, either clothed or nude. After World War I, images of women were influenced by changes in society and in fashion brought

about by designers such as Coco Chanel. Women were now depicted wearing sporting clothes or pants, short skirts, and bobbed, short hair.

Motifs drawn from foreign and ancient cultures were everywhere. The impact of Oriental design, especially Japanese, can be seen in the simplicity of line and the use of bright color combinations. The rediscovery of the tomb of King Tut in Egypt in 1922 sent shock waves of Egyptian imagery through all areas of Art Deco design, with the wholesale borrowing of Egyptian design motifs.

Modern Motifs

The Modern phase of Art Deco design and its desire to make a break with the past brought motifs that were more rectilinear, geometric, or Cubist in inspiration. African motifs, which had begun their appearance in the work of some early French Art Deco designers, were seized upon for their linear, abstract vocabulary.

Jazz itself was a favorite subject for decorative artists, and its syncopated rhythms were reflected in urban, off-beat and angular motifs that appeared in sculptural forms, posters, glassware such as "Ruba Rombic," ceramic decoration, and much more.

Other motifs were drawn from ancient architecture: for example, the skyscraper, whose basic form was borrowed from the "ziggurat" tower and Mayan and Aztec temples, became perhaps the most singularly American Art Deco motif in decorative arts. The stepped-back form was reflected in everything from the "Skyscraper Furniture" of Paul Frankl, to finials on forks. By the end of the era, the skyscraper style had been used so often that many architects and designers were bored with it.

Decorative arts can also reflect the architectural devices that emphasized the soaring verticality of buildings. The

The "Jazz Bowl", 1930, by Viktor Schreckengost. Courtesy of the Cowan Pottery Museum, Ohio.

stepped look was sometimes curved into repeating arcs. The Deco "arc ziggurat" looks like scoops of ice cream topping one another, or a stylized cloud formation. Repeating sunburst patterns were also popular. Half-circles radiating out were used to represent sound, telegraph or radio signals, and other invisible forces of modernity such as "progress."

In some instances, the repeating half-circle motif was replaced with repeating mechanical gears or other industrial images, adding to the design's visual connection to industry. The imagery on the Chrysler Building in New York City, for example, is composed of hubcaps and other automobile design components. Radio City Music Hall and Rockefeller Center abound with breathtaking Art Deco design loaded with American design motifs.

The zigzag, lightning bolt, and chevron became popular Art Deco motifs in America, in everything from neon signs to designs on the faces of countertop radios and handles of hairbrushes. A lightning bolt turned on its side could also represent electricity, and was often used on modern kitchen appliances.

Streamline Motifs

Motifs and forms suggesting movement, speed, or the machine, were the hallmarks of this phase of Art Deco. As even household appliances began to be produced in

"Wisdom," a sculptural relief by Lee Lawrie over the main entrance of the RCA Building, Rockefeller Center. Photo by Robert Four.

a Streamline style, Modernism lost some of its right angles to curved corners and teardrop shapes. Geometric design became aerodynamic design, greatly influenced by the new design for trains, ocean liners and cars. One of the finest styles of roadside diners manufactured during the period was called the "Sterling Streamliner," and different train companies in America launched one "Streamliner" after another.

Generally only simple motifs, such as three parallel "speed lines," are seen on Streamline objects. Often the most decorative element on this era's appliances is the applied company logo. This phase of Art Deco was the

most devoid of ornamentation; little, if any, applied ornamentation was used, and the form of the object itself carried the visual impact.

"Speed Chair" by Paul Frankl, ca. 1933. Courtesy of Modernism Gallery, FL.

Art Deco Animals

Art Deco animals are typically exotic, sleek, and fast: antelopes, gazelles, deer, horses, and greyhounds (and not only the ones in American bus terminals). Antelopes and gazelles were everywhere; leaping across metalwork by Edgar Brandt, prancing on the poster for the 1925 Paris Exposition, grazing around a bowl of Steuben crystal, and animating department store pottery.

A favorite family of animals was the big cats: tigers, panthers, jaguars, and leopards, which were more exotic than endangered at the time. Their sleek, graceful forms lent themselves to sculpture in bronze or ceramic. They were so popular that they continued to be made as inexpensive ceramics that lurked behind low-slung couches and under cocktail tables for decades.

Parakeets, parrots, doves, and other smaller birds were used for decorating vases, were perched on the frames of mirrors, or were incorporated into ceramic design. In American architecture and design, the eagle was trans-

Poster for the 1925 Paris Expo by Robert Bonfils. Author's collection. Photo by Robert Four.

formed: its already angular beak and flat head naturally lent itself to the Modern angular style. Its wings and feathers were set straight back, again in a stepped pattern. In Tropical Deco, flamingoes, herons, and pelicans standing or in flight became part of the popular design menagerie.

Some animals appeared more urbane and sophisticated than ever. Penguins, with their natural "tuxedos," and sometimes complete with top hat and cane, became a favorite "cocktail hour" motif. As the Art Deco style spread internationally, native animals made their appearances in the architecture and design of other countries. For example, stylized elephants adorn the best Art Deco building in Cape Town, South Africa, whereas in Australia, black swans abound.

The Decline of Art Deco Motifs

The popularity of some Art Deco symbols and motifs, and of bold angular lines and graphics waned rapidly when they began to be used more and more in Nazi and Fascist propaganda art. The Modern style, in some eyes, was a Germanic style, and therefore was associated with the Third Reich. In fact, American design had been influenced by the Bauhaus, Wiener Werkstätte, and dozens of immigrants who had come to this country before the War. Just as cans of sauerkraut were taken down from the shelves and replaced by "Liberty Cabbage," the German influence in American design was ignored or denied well into the 1950s.

In the 1940s, when Biomorphism and other postwar design styles replaced Art Deco, form, ornamentation, and motifs changed again. Chairs and other objects took on the shapes of amoebas or, some say, "potato chips." While still streamlined for mass production, organic forms replaced mechanistic ones. One of the most recognizable images of the new "Atomic Era" is a George Nelson wall clock that transforms the Art Deco sunburst pattern into the radiating shape of a molecule or a planetary system.

Materials and Techniques

Knowing the materials that are used in Art Deco design can help a collector evaluate a piece. The intrinsic value of some materials can greatly enhance the price. Also, for the collector, it is important to recognize the materials used in order to avoid deception. For example, onyx bases on clocks and statues can be passed off on the unwary as marble. Early decorative statues used bronze and ivory, but the later ones and imitations used "ivorene," a composition plastic. No shiny brass telephones existed before 1950. Today, when numerous fakes and reproductions of Art Deco designs are on the market, knowing the materials can help you avoid both well-made replicas and poorly-made imitations of the real thing.

Exotic Materials

Early Art Deco artists continued to work in traditional woods and other materials and, like the Art Nouveau artists before them, they displayed a love of exotic materials, which their rich clients could afford. Materials such as silver and gold, inlaid mother of pearl, precious and semi-precious stones, hand-applied lacquer, and enamel were used.

French designers in both the early Art Deco and Art Nouveau periods imported quantities of macassar ebony and ivory. The rarity of these materials today makes it hard to believe they were available in abundance at the time. In fact, at one time the Belgian government held contests to encourage artists to use the tons of ivory being brought back from the Congo. These contests greatly helped increase the popularity of ivory for household items such as brushes and combs, as well as for sculpture in ivory or bronze and ivory (called chryselephantine), which bring some of the highest prices of any Art Deco decorative objects

Today, if you purchase a bronze and ivory statue (or any other object using real ivory), you may encounter problems if you plan to ship it to one of the many countries now banning ivory importation, including the United States. The same restrictions apply to other materials from endangered animals such as crocodile skin and tortoise shell.

Furniture Materials

In France, furniture makers used native sycamore, oak and walnut, as well as more exotic burled woods, zebrawood, amboyna, amaranth, olive wood, rosewood, violet wood, Rio palissandre, palm wood, and a host of others. These gave artists a wide choice for the color, texture, and grain of furniture, using inlays and veneers to create Art Deco patterns. In some of these woods, the grain itself is so bold that it can be seen across a room, adding greatly to the visual impact of the piece.

In 1925 Bauhaus designer Marcel Breuer pioneered the use of steel tubing for furniture, "updating" the bentwood designs of the Vienna Secession, and leading to the later use of tubular chrome. As the use of metal and industrial materials in furniture spread, it was at first met with shock or laughter.

But there was no turning back the clock. The world was rapidly changing, and today we recognize that these industrial materials were used with great genius by the Moderns. Their work was suited to industrial production, and, for designers like Le Corbusier and Robert Mallet-Stevens, these easily mass-produced materials supported their social philosophy and politics as well as their design goals.

In America, tubular steel in furniture would soon be replaced by even cheaper materials more suited to mass production, such as chrome and spun aluminum. These materials were used to great effect by designers such as Wolfgang Hoffmann and Warren McArthur.

Early Scandinavian designers such as Alvar Aalto created streamlined designs in bent wood which would influence American designers in the 1940s, such as Charles and Rae Eames, in their designs of bent plywood, and later, plastic molded chairs.

Lacquer and Enamel

The use of lacquer began in earnest with the arrival in Paris in 1918 of the Japanese artist Sugawara. His influence on two noted designers, Eileen Gray and Jean Dunand, to whom he taught the ancient art, would make lacquer an overwhelmingly popular technique.

White was the only color that could not be produced by lacquer, and Dunand discovered the art of using crushed egg shells to create his patterns. Lacquered pieces were often rendered in geometric red, black, and silver designs, a favorite Deco color combination. Other artists began working in lacquer on everything: small and large boxes, panels, and furniture.

Later, fast-drying industrial lacquer would replace the painstaking layering process, meaning that more and more items could be produced in "lacquer" finishes. Enameling was also a popular technique for enriching vases and other decorative objects. In the 1930s, industrial baked enamel finishes became popular on household appliances.

Metal

Traditional metals, like bronze and wrought iron, continued to be used. As before, wrought iron was used extensively in architectural detail, and bronze as a medium for sculpture. However, perhaps due to the genius of designers such as Edgar Brandt, wrought iron became popular in tables, lamps, and other furnishings. Glass and metal artists, such as Brandt and Daum, collaborated to create stunning lighting fixtures, showing off the other's talents even more.

Precious metals such as copper, silver and gold maintained their value, but were used in different ways. New metal-crafting techniques also came along, such as autogenous welding, which allowed two different metals, such as bronze and silver, to be welded together. In America, chrome and aluminum would soon replace the use of other metals in all manner of household decorations, cocktail shakers, and kitchenware. While one might jump to the conclusion that chrome items would never have the value of silver, certain Art Deco chrome cocktail shakers can bring more today at auction than a Jean Puiforcat silver tea set.

New Materials and Techniques

In the 1930s, mass production brought with it the advent of kitchenware that was made from machine-produced, highly polished chrome, and toward the end of the period, aluminum became increasingly popular. Ceramics were able to be fired and glazed in one step. Wood veneers replaced inlaid wood, and cheap woods were hidden under industrial enamels. Whole walls of houses were constructed with glass block.

Radios, kitchen utensils, household decorations, ashtrays, and production furniture were made using materials such as chrome or nickel-plated steel, painted base metals, mirrored glass, and a wide range of trademarked plastics, such as Catalin and Bakelite. These materials were often decorated through a variety of methods in bright, jazzy colors. Art Deco had become a dime store dream: cheap and cheerful enough to get us through the Depression. ◼

3
TODAY'S MARKET

The term "Art Deco" was coined in 1968, and the first major museum retrospective of the style took place in 1970–1971. The late 1960s and early 1970s saw a "first wave" of Art Deco collecting attract avant-garde collectors, such as Barbra Streisand and Elton John. The first Art Deco preservation organization, the Miami Design Preservation League, was founded in 1976.

A second important resurgence in Art Deco collecting accompanied major museum exhibitions of the late 1980s, focusing primarily on American Art Deco: "High Styles" at the Whitney Museum in 1986; "The Machine Age in America" at the Brooklyn Museum the same year; and "American Art Deco" at the Renwick Gallery in 1987. Specialized shows and fairs, such as Sanford Smith's

"Modernism" in New York began to spring up in 1986, and the market expanded significantly.

Throughout the 1990s, the market for Art Deco grew and diversified. Numerous books on various aspects of Art Deco appeared, and specialized museum exhibitions abounded. Many new collecting areas emerged, and scholarly research helped identify and differentiate the relative importance of period designers. The number of shows focusing on Art Deco design annually in the United States now hovers at about a dozen, with many others overseas.

Today, Art Deco is enjoying a third major renaissance of popularity. As we entered into the 21st century, early 20th-century design took on an added historic importance for collectors and museums. Though the overall level of the market has been somewhat dampened by the economic downturn since the tragedies of September 11, 2001, collecting Art Deco is more widely popular now than at any other time in history. Many works are still achieving record prices, and all indications suggest that the market will continue its climb.

Beginning in 2003, a major museum exhibition "Art Deco, 1910–1939," which started at the Victoria and Albert Museum in London, has been touring to Canada and the United States. The first major museum exhibition in more than fifteen years, accompanied by an outstanding new book of the same title, will undoubtedly add more fuel to the fire of Art Deco's expanding popularity. (See the Bibliography in the Resource Guide for dates and more information.)

- **Record Prices and Collectible Values**—The record price for an Art Deco object at auction is shared by two works by French designers: "Tardieu," a chromed metal and lacquer desk, by Jacques-Émile Ruhlmann for the Salon des Artistes Décorateurs, 1929, and "L'Oasis," a monumental iron and brass five-panel decorative screen by Edgar Brandt, circa 1924. Both of these objects sold for $1,876,000 each in separate auctions in 2000 at Christie's New York. What has emerged most strongly in the market over the past decade are the works of American Modernist designers. Finally getting their due vis-à-vis their French counterparts, record prices for designers such as Paul Frankl, Donald Deskey, Gilbert Rohde, and many others have been established. Notwithstanding the sometimes staggering prices, because the Art Deco style was also reflected in many mass produced objects through the 1930s, good examples of the style can still be acquired by beginning collectors for under $100.

- **Collecting Categories and Collectors**—Because the Art Deco style was so widely applied, the field encompasses an extremely broad variety of collecting categories, and thus appeals to numerous collectors. From high-end French glass such as Lalique and Daum, to Depression glass by Anchor Hocking; from fine silver to cocktail shakers; from fine art objects to plastic radios and industrial design; from fine jewelry by Tiffany to Bakelite bracelets; from Belgian ceramics by Boch Frères and colorful English tea sets by Clarice Cliff, to American pottery such as Roseville and Cowan. From the refined high styles of the Paris Exposition of 1925 to the wildly popular Jazz and Hollywood styles of the 1930s, there is something for every taste and every pocketbook. Large-scale production of objects in the Art Deco style took place in the U.S. from the end of the 1920s through the beginning of World War II. Because of the variety of collecting areas, I would estimate that there are more than 250,000 active collectors of Art Deco in the United States. Those who have at least one or a few good examples of Art Deco in their collections must easily number more than one million.

- **Auctions**—All of the major auction houses in the United States—such as Bonhams & Butterfields, Christie's, Doyle, Phillips, de Pury & Luxembourg, Skinner, and Sotheby's—host auctions which focus on 20th century design. Swann Galleries hosts several poster auctions annually that include Art Deco, including dedicated auctions of "Modernist Posters." Numerous smaller auction houses have emerged as important players in the field as well, including: David Rago with his partner John Sollo; LA Modern Auctions, which was once associated with Butterfields; Treadway Galleries; and Wright in Chicago. Regional auction houses such as Ivey-Selkirk in St. Louis are also claiming some of the auction action. These sales often combine Art Deco with other 20th-century design styles such as Art Nouveau, Arts and Crafts, or Mid-Century Modern, exposing even more individuals to the style.

- **Shows**—Once banned from most antique shows as "kitsch," today there is a growing number of dedicated 20th-century design shows. The New York "Modernism" show, started in 1986 and taking place each November, gave rise to a host of other such shows across the country. Today, Modernism shows take place annually in Miami (January), Palm Springs (March), Chicago (April), Los Angeles (May), and Winnetka (November). Other 20th-century shows and Art Deco expos take place in New York (March, October, and November), San Francisco (June and December), Washington, D.C. (June), Cincinnati (February/March), and elsewhere. Abroad, high-end Modernism-style shows also take place in London, Amsterdam, and Copenhagen. Today, most large antique shows include some dealers in Art Deco and modern design styles.

- **Art Deco Societies**—Starting with the Miami Design Preservation League in 1976, Art Deco societies and 20th-century preservation organizations have proliferated. Today, twenty-five Art Deco societies in Australia (4), Canada (3), New Zealand (2), South Africa (2), the United Kingdom (1), and the United States (13) are united under the banner of the International Coalition of Art Deco Societies (ICADS). While membership bases are relatively modest (from 100 to 1000), most of the societies publish newsletters and have a Web presence. A complete listing thereof is included in the Resource Guide.

- **Specialized Dealers**—Specialized dealers exist across the United States. Many Art Deco dealers also carry Mid-Century and other 20th-century design styles, but we estimate that, including all categories of Art Deco collecting, there are approximately 350–400 dealers nationwide. The general market has moved greatly toward Mid-Century design, due in part to the fact that there are large quantities of mass-produced designs from this period available, whereas better Art Deco materials are both harder to find and more expensive overall. The Resource Guide includes some fifty recommended U.S. dealers coast to coast, many of whom also carry Mid-Century design.

- **Scholarship and Museums**—Art Deco is one of the most popular subjects for coffee-table and design books. In the past five years alone, almost sixty titles have been published or reissued focusing on specific Art Deco periods, designers, architecture of various countries and cities, Art Deco silver, jewelry, fashion, furniture, lighting, textiles, carpets, and even Art Deco hairstyles! The Bibliography highlights many of the books which are still available, and can help you identify an in-depth sourcebook in the area that interests you the most. The best volumes are often produced in association with important museum shows, where curators often contribute groundbreaking scholarship. Several museums have outstanding collections of Art Deco and other Modernist design, and we have again listed a select number of American museums in the Resource Guide.

- **Internet**—Access to information about Art Deco has never been greater due to the advent of the World Wide Web. Of course, many collectors today actively add to their collections through sites such as eBay. Many dealers who used to only do shows or sell by appointment now have active e-commerce sites for Art Deco, and some have even closed their retail operations in favor of operating solely on the Internet. Today, most of the auction houses, dealers, shows, societies, and museums included in the Resource Guide have Web sites you can visit.

As you can see, today's market for Art Deco is highly charged, extensive, and complex. Getting to know the resources available and exploring the entire field to the best of your ability will help you focus your collecting and build your expertise. ◼

4

A KEY TO COLLECTIBLE VALUE

Many factors come into play when determining the value of Art Deco furnishings, objects, works on paper, collectibles, and industrial design. Of course, in many ways, value is determined by the market: auction records, average prices in the marketplace, or just the price that a collector is willing to pay for an item for his or her collection. Below are some of the overall key factors which affect collectible value in the Art Deco field.

Design Achievement

While there are exceptions, works by recognized designers will always have a generally higher value than those by lesser-known makers or anonymous designs.

Designers such as Jacques-Émile Ruhlmann, Edgar Brandt, Donald Deskey, Paul Frankl, René Lalique, Charles Catteau, Clarice Cliff, Jean Puiforcat, Norman Bel Geddes, A. M. Cassandre, Henry Dreyfuss, and numerous others are widely recognized as innovators whose work stands head and shoulders above the work of their contemporaries.

Most designers of this stature were considered important contributors to the world of design during their lifetimes, and most of them produced significantly large bodies of work with consistently high quality to earn that recognition. However, "unknown" artists today can become a celebrated, "rediscovered" artist tomorrow. The past twenty years have brought to light numerous designers who were previously unrecognized for their design achievements, so one also has to use your instincts.

Design Authentication

In typical auction catalogue language, some designs have evidence that they are *by* a specific designer, some are *attributed* to the designer and, others, lacking verification, are simply considered to be *in the style of* or *in the manner of* the designer. These indications can greatly affect the value of any work on the market. A dealer might feel "certain" that a piece is the work of a specific designer but, unless there is a signature, written evidence, or substantiating research or documentation, then it is really only an *attribution*.

Signatures, stamps, marks, patent numbers and other means that collectors rely on to help authenticate a piece, can also add value to a work in some cases. However, this whole area can also be confusing in the world of Art Deco and, in some cases, it can also be used as a means to defraud collectors.

Few decorative arts, with the exception of some studio pieces and special commissions, were signed by the designer, as an artist would sign a canvas. In those rare instances, you might hear a signature described as "hand signed," "hand-painted," a "pencil signature," or an "original signature." In some fields, such as rare books, when an item is described as "signed by the author," or "signed by the artist," this generally means "hand signed." In these instances, a signature can add significant market value.

Most often, when a work is described as "signed" in the decorative arts, it implies some other means of applying the artist's signature or name to the piece. Signatures can be cast, incised, etched, molded, stamped, or printed. Sometimes descriptions offered by dealers and others will be precise: "an ink-stamped signature," or "an etched signature." Sometimes the piece will simply be referred to as "signed."

In the world of posters, "signed" usually means that the artist signed the lithographic stone, for example, signed the original design that was later printed in multiple copies. Henry Dreyfuss did not hand-sign his now famous Thermos; a "facsimile" signature was stamped into the metal. Russel Wright did not hand-sign all of the "American Modern" ceramic pieces he designed—they were ink-stamped with his signature.

In instances like these, while the signature can increase value over anonymous pieces by authenticating the work, the signature in itself does not add any significant value.

In each field, designers used different marks, stamps, and other means of identifying their work. In fine silver, each country used a different "hallmark," or stamp, to identify its production. Industrial manufacture often carries a trademark, logo, patent number, or other means of identification. However, even a patent number is no guarantee of authenticity, for example, modern Korean replicas of Art Deco telephones are often stamped with the original patent numbers.

It is up to you to get to know the marks and signatures of the fields you are most interested in to help you avoid deception. The Art Deco field is so broad that we cannot provide that information in this small volume, but you will find it in the other books to which we refer you, given the collecting area.

Quality of the Design

Within a designer's body of work, there will always be some pieces that are prized more than others for their design achievement. Even when a designer reaches the ranks of "the best," not all of their work will be considered the best examples of their style or use of materials. This is also true for the output of manufacturers for entire collecting fields or for specific collecting areas.

For example, furniture designer Paul Frankl created innovative studio work early in his career, but he also went on to design pieces for machine production, and even designed some popular rattan furniture that appears frequently on the market today. While his production furniture may still be considered a Good or Better example of his work, his earlier pieces and special commissions will always be more highly regarded, and have a higher value.

Manufacturers, such as Chase Brass and Copper, produced a wide variety of items, a handful of which are considered the finest examples of Chase design. Many pieces were created by notable designers. Determinations such as these can only be made by comparing a wide variety of works by a particular designer or in a particular collecting field. This means you have to study the market or go to shows and auctions and handle the material.

Other factors will affect the judgment of the quality of a piece, for example, whether the work was handmade or machine-produced, or based on the materials from which it is made.

Generally speaking, when we say in this volume that a piece represents a "Good," "Better," or "Best" example of a designer's or manufacturer's work, we mean:

Good
A collectible example of the Art Deco style or the designer's work, but not really unique or distinguished. It is perhaps unsigned, unidentifiable by maker or designer, or the date of manufacture unknown. If maker is known, it is perhaps one of the many mass-produced American or European designs of the period, commonly found or still readily available on the general antiques and collectibles market.

Better
A well-executed example of the Art Deco style or the designer's work. It is distinguished in some way by its orig-

inality, application of materials, or technique; identified maker, designer or manufacturer, perhaps with original label; perhaps produced in a small edition, numbered and signed, or details finished by hand; if mass-produced, recognized as one of the best examples of design for its category; not easily found.

Best

An example showing the finest attributes of the Art Deco style or the designer's work. It has a known maker or designer, with signature or mark and known provenance; recognized as an important work by a leading designer or maker; highly original or unique in use of materials, design and overall aesthetic; handmade, perhaps one-of-a-kind, or a rare surviving example of a small edition; rarely seen.

Rarity

Generally speaking, if a piece is *truly* rare—a special commission, a known small edition, one of a few surviving examples—it will attract more interest, and someone will pay more to have it.

Even though much of the early Art Deco production was handmade, while later work tends to be machine-made, some mass-produced items are today very rare. Take, for example, Catalin radios. While they were machine-made and mass-produced, in reality very few survived and, in some cases, only one or two examples of a particular radio are known to exist. Notice we say "known to exist"; it is always possible that more will be found.

In addition, rarity alone will not necessarily increase value unless other key factors also exist. For example, one might purchase an apparently handmade lacquered box at a flea market, and the dealer will assure you it is "probably one-of-a-kind." Unless the designer can be authenticated or it is a superb example, it will have no more value than hundreds of other anonymous "one-of-a-kind" lacquered boxes on the market.

Intrinsic Value of Materials

In some areas of Art Deco collecting, the intrinsic value of the materials used will play a role in helping to determine value. This is most obvious with precious gems and metals: gold, silver, platinum, diamonds, sapphires, and the like. Furniture can also have a value based on its materials: rare woods, ivory inlay, and other precious materials will always have a greater intrinsic value than chrome-plated steel or plastic. However, in the collecting world, usually only a small portion of an item's value is based on the intrinsic value of the materials used, and far more weight is given to other considerations. For example, you'll pay more for a Norman Bel Geddes "Manhattan Cocktail Set" in chrome than you will for many diamond brooches, and some Catalin plastic radios can cost more than a zebrawood table by a French designer.

Subject

In certain collecting areas, the subject being depicted can impact the value of a piece. For example, in the world of Art Deco posters, (artist, condition, etc.) trains, aviation themes, ocean liners, and cabaret or theater subjects will generally bring more than product posters for items like cough drops, shoes, or toothpaste. In bronze and ivory sculpture, exotic figures of women dancers, performers such as Josephine Baker, and similar subjects command higher prices that sculptures of children or animals. Certain Art Deco subjects have become icons of the era, such as jazz.

Condition

The condition of a piece has a lot to do with its value on the market, but you'll notice we've listed it last. Condition is judged in different ways in different collecting fields and, often, condition will be considered less important than the reputation of the designer and the rarity of the piece. In fact, the more important a piece is in other ways, the less important the condition.

That being said, condition should certainly be a factor in determining what you are willing or not willing to pay for a specific piece, given that you may have to spend time and money restoring, repairing, or cleaning a piece. It is also important to know what can and cannot be repaired, or what repairs might still be visible when completed and detract from the value.

The term "mint" should be used only to refer to items that are in the same condition as they were when originally made. In some Art Deco collecting fields, "mint" condition pieces are still found on the market, for example, a set of Chase Chrome in its original box. However, in most cases, Art Deco pieces have been used, if only to a limited degree, and the term "mint" does not apply.

Bottom line: It is always best to purchase items in "excellent" or "fine" condition, or in the very best condition that you can find them. This will help ensure the value of your collection over time. For very rare pieces, sometimes a collector will lower his standards and purchase an item that is only in "good" condition. However, a common mistake beginning collectors make is to purchase an item in "good" condition because they think it is rare, only to find out later that it is still available on the market elsewhere in much better condition. You will also see many items on the market that are really in very bad condition. In most cases, it's best to just pass up these items. ◼

5
FAKES ALERT!

Unfortunately, the revitalization of interest in Art Deco in the last thirty years has also seen a flood of both expensive and cheaply produced reproductions and forgeries on the market. Today's collector has to be either very wary or very well-educated in his or her chosen area when purchasing Art Deco objects from sellers they do not know.

Remember that Art Deco is no longer an unknown style and, most of the time, sellers and others will know exactly what an object is worth. In collecting Art Deco, the best rule of thumb to follow is that if the price looks too good to be true, it probably isn't!

Furniture

There are elegant reproductions of furniture today using almost exactly the same materials as early the French designers. One company was producing a noted Ruhlmann desk for about $10,000, the original now brings in six figures.

In addition, because the Art Deco era was not that long ago, some companies are still issuing or licensing the designs they produced more than fifty years ago. For example: Josef Hoffmann's bentwood "Fledermaus" chairs; Mies van der Rohe's chairs, such as the "Brno Chair," still sold through Knoll; Cassina's licensed reproduction of a famous chair by Le Corbusier; and Nessen Lighting reissues of designs by Walter von Nessen. Design America has reissued Paul Frankl designs for chairs and sofas. Even 1930s American furniture in chrome and aluminum is being reproduced. We hasten to add that all of the above pieces are being reproduced with very high-quality materials and standards but they are still not the original production.

If you are in doubt, don't be afraid to ask. If you don't fully trust the person with whom you are dealing, pass it up. If your love of Art Deco is really just for decorating your home, then go ahead and purchase a 2001 wall sconce rather than the 1930 original. It may serve your needs better, but don't expect it to have any long-term value on the collecting market.

Decorative Sculpture

Despite frequents fraud warnings, recastings and reproductions of Art Deco, Art Nouveau, Remington, and other statues proliferate on the market today, sometimes sold side-by-side with originals. Since the early 1970s, it has been the hardest-hit area in Art Deco collecting. In many cases, the recastings are very good, and even experts have problems detecting fakes with chemically aged patina, real ivory, foundry marks, and attention to detail. Because most of these designs are in the public domain, nothing can prevent reissues, and about five foundries in the U.S. put out large quantities over the past thirty years.

Some are more obvious: cheaply cast, patinated colors, bases that look too new, signatures spelled incorrectly, ivory faked by the use of "ivorine" and a plastic that does not yellow or age like ivory. Unfortunately, some of the fakes smuggled in from Hong Kong before the ban on ivory used real ivory and were exquisite reproductions, even slipping through the showrooms of a few reputable auction houses unnoticed.

A reputable auction house or seller will describe original bronzes as "cast *from* a model by the artist" and later re-castings as "cast *after* a model by the artist." Again, price alone might help you spot a fake, as original bronze and ivory statues can sell for tens of thousands of dollars at auction.

Demetre H. Chiparus is the most frequently faked. Many of his works were for Etling, and originals will almost always carry a foundry name and his signature etched in the marble. Look closely at the fine details: You should be able to make out the fingernails on the fingers. However, that alone may not be enough to help you spot a fake. Some of the other fakes most frequently seen on the market are Marcel Bouraine, Claire Jeanne Roberte Colinet, Jean Descomps, Pierre Le Faguays, Joseph Lorenzl, Ferdinand Preiss and Bruno Zach.

Silver and Chrome

Sterling silver is difficult to fake, but again it is best to buy from a reputable seller. Some of the fine silver designs of the day have been remanufactured, such as the Christofle coffee set from the *Normandie*, but these are often sold registered and numbered and, from what we've seen, are worth the retail prices asked. Again, it is best to get to know the maker's marks, country hall-marks, and other stamps used on fine silver. Even tiny earrings will usually carry a silver mark.

Chrome and other metals, which were used prolifically for housewares, trays and serving sets, cocktail shakers, coffee sets, and the like are less a target for forgeries than they are for reproductions. The resurgence of popularity of the martini means you can now buy a replica of the famous Napier penguin cocktail shaker for $29.95, versus the original which can sell for $2,500 or more. The real problem with all of these reproductions will probably come twenty years from now after they've been used and sold in garage sales.

Glass

A frequent deception in glass is forgery of a signature or mark, so inspect pieces carefully, and get to know the mark of the designer or maker you want to collect. A well-done fake signature is hard to detect, and the best bet if you are collecting signed glass is to arm yourself with a scholarly book in which signatures of glassmakers are reproduced. One of the best of these is *Glass: Art Nouveau to Art Deco*, by Victor Arwas.

Another word of caution about collecting glass: Repairs and damage are generally hard to hide in glass, but sometimes a chip on a rim is repaired by the entire rim being cut down. A seller may "forget" to tell you if there is a small chip or crack, so run your fingers carefully over the surfaces and the rim.

There is an abundance of contemporary glass that imitates Art Deco styles. In addition, artists such as René Lalique were imitated in their own day. Etling, Sabino, and other manufacturers produced Lalique-like frosted glass, which is both collectible and, in some cases, superb. American imitators included Consolidated Lamp and Glass Company and Phoenix Glass Company in the 1930s. Today, these makers are collected on their own merits. The only deception is when an unscrupulous seller offers these or any other frosted glass piece as Lalique.

Lalique glass can bring such high prices that it is easy to see why it is a favorite target for reproductions and forgeries. Also, with very rare exceptions, Lalique glass is marked, so be wary of someone offering you "unsigned Lalique." There was also a rash of well-made reproductions of Lalique and other famous glass makers emanating most probably from Brazil. To skirt charges of fraud, some of these crooks simply misspelled "Lallique" [sic].

Ceramics

Some of the same warnings given above about the condition of glass also apply to ceramics. It may be easy to spot a chip in a color ceramic glazing, but it is sometimes impossible to tell if the glazing has been repaired. Watch for brightly colored pottery that has been simply overpainted to hide problems. Generally, the overpainted area will be either a little too dull or a little too glossy to match the original glaze.

Hairline cracks are harder to see in ceramics than in glass because you can't see them by holding them up to the light. Tap the ceramic lightly but sharply with your finger, and if there is a dull thud instead of a ring, the ceramic may well have a hairline crack somewhere.

Some Art Deco dinnerwares, such as Hall China and Fiesta are being reproduced. The Hall China Company in Ohio is casting pieces from the original molds, and the new ones are just as nice as the originals. The best way to tell the difference is by knowing the company trademark, stamped on the bottom of the piece, which has changed over time. In addition, today's Hall, with its pastel shades of pink, blue, and white is also quite different from its original production in Chinese Red, Delphinium Blue, Lettuce Green, and other colors.

The same "color theory" holds true somewhat for Homer Laughlin's Fiestaware, produced from 1936 through 1972, and reintroduced in 1986. To the original colors of red, blue, yellow, green, ivory and turquoise were added in 1938. Red ceased production in 1943, when the uranium oxide needed to create it went to wartime use, but it returned in 1959. After World War II, new colors were added, and the 1986 colors were apricot, rose, cobalt blue, black, and white. A sea-mist green was added in 1991. Confused? Then buy only through a reputable seller.

Ceramic reproductions and imitations of Art Deco abound: lamps, vases, teapots, statues, ashtrays, bookends, clocks, and more, selling in all price ranges. In fairness, it should be noted that *most* of these reproductions are plainly marked with the names of the manufacturers. However, that does not stop people from trying to sell them as vintage. In some cases, all it takes is the peeling off of a label. It is up to you to know the difference.

Posters
Before World War II, most posters were printed lithographically, and it is these that most sellers and collectors today refer to as "vintage." A lithograph is printed

from a stone or metal plate. The design is drawn on the surface with a greasy medium, and the entire surface is dampened with water. Since grease repels water, when a greasy colored ink is then applied, it adheres only to the drawing. Paper is laid down, and the whole thing is run through a scraper that presses the colored ink into the paper.

Under a jeweler's lens or a very strong magnifying glass, lithographs will generally have an evenness in their colored areas. In lithographs, lines often look like they have been drawn by a crayon, and spatter areas look like spattered paint.

In photo offset, a photograph is taken of the original art and turned into negatives. The negatives are used to photochemically etch into the plate from which the poster will be printed. To make etching possible, the negative must be turned into a series of very tiny, regular dots in neat, straight lines that often can't be seen with the naked eye. Use a jeweler's lens or a very strong magnifying glass to look at any photograph in your daily newspaper, and you will see the dots in straight lines (called a "dot matrix") of photo offset printing.

The copyrights on many vintage posters ran out long ago. Anyone with a printing press can print and distribute for sale a vast number of poster titles by notable Art Deco artists. Hundreds of lithographic posters have been reproduced by photo offset by commercial poster publishers. These are fairly easy to spot using the method above.

Unfortunately, in the past decade, a number of companies have emerged that reproduce lithographic posters or use digital imaging to reproduce posters, thus eliminating the photo offset dot screen. These replicas are so good that they can fool most people, and many are even being printed at the exact same size as the original, doubling the confusion.

Industrial Design
The newest area of problems and potential problems is Industrial Design. Prices on some of the collectible industrial designs of the period have climbed, spawning reproductions.

For example, Walter Dorwin Teague's blue mirrored glass Sparton "Bluebird" radio, was reproduced and sold at $250. One magazine, which was actually applauding the reproduction, headlined their story "Deco on the Outside—Sony on the Inside." Fake Catalin radios are on the market, and most recently someone has begun reproducing the so-called "piston" lamp by Pattyn Products that adorns the cover of this book.

In Industrial Design, perhaps the easiest thing to look for is typical wear, rust, discoloration, and other signs of age that tell you an object is old. If it is shiny and new, but the seller claims it is an original, it may also have been rechromed or repainted. Look for makers' marks and metal plates with patent numbers. However, some replicas, such as telephones, have been issued with the original patent numbers stamped into them and reproductions of the well-known, but anonymously designed blue glass and chrome airplane lamp have been on the market so long that they often show enough wear to pass as the originals. ◼

6

FURNISHINGS

Furniture design reflected the profound transitions that were taking place in fashion, style, and society in the 1920s and 1930s. Furnishings for both homes and offices were transformed not only by new design ideas, but by new lifestyles, technical advances, and new materials and inventions. The evolution of the Art Deco style from the stylized yet flowery French Art Deco, through the Germanic, geometric Moderne phase of the style, and into the final Streamline style is highly evident in the design of furnishings.

Furniture

Tradition-loving French *ébénistes*, or cabinetmakers, while abandoning the overly ornamental Art Nouveau, still used highly refined materials. Their very trade gets its name from *ébène de macassar*, or macassar ebony.

Other rare and expensive woods that were popular included Brazilian palissandre, rosewood, palm wood, zebrawood, mahogany, amboyna, amaranth, and violet wood. Materials and finishes, such as hand-applied lacquer, *bronze doré* or gilt-bronze, ivory, mother of pearl and tortoise shell were also frequently used. Wrought-iron eventually came to surpass bronze in popularity for furnishings, due in part to the talents of the artists who chose the medium.

Another favorite material was *galuchat*, the skin of a dogfish, specially treated to be used and tooled like leather on desktops and other furniture and decorations. Today, you'll often hear *galuchat* called sharkskin, and it is also substituted as a term for *peau de chagrin*, which translates as "shagreen." Parchment was also used to cover expensive furniture.

There were numerous notable designers of furniture during the early French Art Deco period. For the most part, their work is highly prized and highly priced today. Often, they created their furniture for wealthy clients who commissioned them to design unique pieces.

French designers who are at the top of the collecting market include Jacques-Émile Ruhlmann, Pierre Legrain, Eugene Printz, Armand-Albert Rateau, Jules Leleu, Louis Süe and André Mare and their "Compagnie des Arts Français," Andre Groult, Clément Rousseau, André Domin and Marcel Genevrière's company, "Dominique," and the master lacquer artist Jean Dunand. A few designers, such as Louis Majorelle, successfully made the transition from Art Nouveau to Art Deco.

Others who are well-known with strong prices include Maurice Dufrène, Jean-Michel Frank, Paul Vera, Clément Mère, Léon Jallot, Paul Follot, Paul Iribe, and Paul Poiret and his firm, "Atelier Martine." This list is by no means exhaustive, and collectors who are interested in early French Art Deco furniture design should delve into such books as Alastair Duncan's *Art Deco Furniture: The French Designers*. Dealers who truly specialize in this rare early material are few and far between, and we recommend Maison Gérard, in New York City, and Calderwood Gallery, in Philadelphia, as outstanding sources for the early French designers.

The highest quality works, which auction houses like to call "important" pieces, are often only found in museums and leading private collections and rarely appear on the open market.

Overall, Jacques-Émile Ruhlmann remains the undisputed master of the Art Deco furniture market. He was known as a maker of luxury furniture, and his work was expensive even in his own times. He received numerous commissions from wealthy individuals, as well as from the French government for the decoration of embassies, town halls, and luxury ocean liners such as the *Île-de-France*.

The world auction record for a work by Ruhlmann is for a 1929 desk that he entitled "Tardieu," which was created for the 1929 Salon des Artistes Décorateurs. It sold for $1,876,000 in December, 2000 at Christie's New York. Ironically, the semi-circular desk is in chromed metal and black lacquer, and reflects much more of a Moderne sensibility than his best-known work.

At press time, this auction record also ties the world auction record for an Art Deco object, with the other being a monumental iron and brass five-panel decorative screen called "L'Oasis," created by the master Edgar Brandt in 1924. The screen set the record of $1,876,000 in June, 2000, also at Christie's New York.

Louis Süe and André Mare were the most traditional designers of the period in many ways, and were influenced by provincial styles. Their Compagnie des Arts Français created dignified furniture that is highly prized today for its refinement and restraint. In many ways, their furniture, clocks, and other furnishings, often carved or decorated with stylized fruit and flowers, are the penultimate reflection of early French Art Deco. A sampling of auction prices for Süe et Mare includes $71,700 for a carved macassar ebony canapé and $26,290 for a pair of black lacquered armchairs, both at Christie's in 2002, and $90,500 for a set of eight macassar ebony dining chairs at the same auction house in 1998.

Jules Leleu is another highly sought-after early French Art Deco designer. Widely commissioned by both individuals and the French government, his furniture designs are re-

strained and elegant. He opened a gallery in Paris in 1924, and was exhibited in the 1925 Paris Exposition. In addition to many notable designs for French embassies around the world, he also created furnishings for many of the ocean liners. His output was truly prolific. Rare, one-of-a-kind commissioned pieces can sell for more than $200,000. Much of his work falls into a mid-range of $10,000 to $30,000 at auction, for example: a pair of ebony and ivory inlaid amboyna side tables sold at Sotheby's New York in 2002 for just over $28,000, while a palissandre dining table and twelve chairs brought more than $31,000 at the same auction house the year prior.

Jean Dunand, influenced by Asian design and artisans, perfected the art of lacquer, and especially eggshell lacquer. The lengthy hand-lacquering process of layer upon layer requires extreme skill and patience if a high-quality finish is to be obtained. However, by the 1930s, lacquer had become mechanized, and industrial lacquers and enamels in design were commonplace. Dunand's works are treasured. For example, a small eggshell lacquer table by Dunand sold for $105,000 in 2001 at Christie's, his lacquered room screens can command five times that amount, and even his eggshell lacquer vases often sell for more than $60,000 at auction.

Cabinet by Jules Leleu, ca. 1927, in Brazilian rosewood with ivory inlay. Courtesy of Calderwood Gallery, PA.

The fashions of the day, inspired by the Ballets Russes Orientalism, also affected furniture design. Just as the previous generation's hoop skirts and crinolines necessitated certain proportions for chairs, the new fashion meant new furniture. To wear an Oriental-inspired robe or long stylish dress with the required casual slinkiness, a low-slung couch or *chaise longue*, literally, "long chair," was needed instead of a straight-backed settee. To go with low chairs, tables became low cocktail or coffee tables. Furniture was redesigned for comfort, including deeper armchairs and dining room tables with a single pedestal instead of legs.

There was a trend for pattern-on-pattern textiles and cushions with long silk tassels. Interior designers paid as much attention to tapestry, curtains, chair covers, and wall hangings as they did to furniture. Fountains, flowers and multi-colored brocades were typical designs, and some have dubbed this a "boudoir style."

Paul Follot used abstract shapes and stylized flowers in textiles to create a rich effect. Follot liked "beautiful" materials and techniques such as marquetry, lacquer, and bronze work. In 1923, he became director of Pomone, the design boutique in the department store Au Bon Marché, and he was in charge of its pavilion at the 1925 Exhibition. He defended the *de luxe* tradition and was opposed to mass-produced furnishings. A pair of gilt armchairs was recently offered on the retail market for $11,000, and a small pedestal table in mahogany was priced at $25,000.

Maurice Dufrène, who in 1904 had been a founding member of the Salon des Artistes Décorateurs, became the director of La Maitrise, the design boutique in the department store Galéries Lafayette. He designed a multitude of furnishings, ceramics, and decorations which were executed by numerous companies. A 49" × 43" oval table by Dufrène with a geometric design was recently offered on the market at $35,000.

These specialized design boutiques in the department stores had a huge impact on furniture design, and their pavilions at the 1925 Paris Exposition were among the most popular. Along with those named above, Claude Lévy, who directed the Primavera workshop at Au Bon

Marché, commissioned numerous designers in all of the decorative arts for their stores.

Even after the use of tubular metal in furniture design gained popularity at the end of the 1920s and early 1930s, some French designers remained loyal to traditional materials, although they often adopted modern form and design. Today, they are gaining increasing recognition and popularity with collectors who enjoy the warmth of wooden furniture.

Included in this category are André Arbus, Ruhlmann's nephew Alfred Porteneuve, Jean Pascaud, Jean Royère, Louis Sognot, and Jacques Adnet, who took over the direction of Süe et Mare's Compagnie des Arts Français in 1928 and remained until 1959. Also sought after are works by René Prou, who succeeded Follot as director of Pomone from 1928 to 1932, and Michel Dufet, whose company Meubles Artistiques Modernes created stunning designs which were produced in series by Le Bucheron. Frank Rogin's excellent showroom in New York City often features works by these and other French designers.

A sampling of recent asking prices on the retail market for these designers have included $18,500 for a fall front secretary by André Arbus; $73,000 for a unique cabinet made of sycamore and parchment also by Arbus; $18,000 for a palissandre (Brazilian rosewood) console by Porteneuve; $45,000 for a commode with its original parchment and gilt wood legs by Pascaud; $22,500 for a cabinet/bookcase by Adnet; and $5,500 for a coffee table in ebony by Sognot.

As should be obvious by these prices, if you intend furnish your home with French Art Deco furniture, the serious prices should be preceded by some serious research into the market. At prices like these, you might want to rely on an experienced consultant, or develop a relationship with a specialized dealer who knows the nuances of the market.

In 1927 metal furniture was first exhibited at the Salon des Artistes Décorateurs. The new furniture designers were greatly influenced by the Bauhaus where, in 1924, Marcel Breuer had introduced the first furniture made with tubular steel, and modular furniture the following year. Sometimes called the "Moderns," they regarded furniture as "interior architecture" or "household equipment." They further simplified the lines, volume, and decoration, making it easier to mass produce and reflecting social and economic changes in the world.

Eileen Gray, who was Irish but worked in Paris, created floor lamps, benches, and tables using asymmetrical designs that echo Cubist patterns. One of the earliest Moderns, her style was also very individual, and she received numerous commissions by forward-thinking collectors of the day. She ranks second only to Dunand in her use of lacquer. Gray's designs are highly coveted. For example, a unique lacquered console table sold at Christie's in 2000 for $534,000.

Thonet began to mass produce tubular steel frames in 1928. Concert halls, restaurants, and other commercial establishments were quick to realize the practicality of the new stacking chair. With the rise of urban centers, especially after the Wall Street crash of 1929, the demand for fine furniture was not as great as the demand for less costly furniture for everyday use by middle-class families.

In 1930, inspired by the Bauhaus and modern theories of Charles Edouard Jeanneret, who called himself Le Corbusier, a number of artists created the Union Des Artistes Modernes (U.A.M.), and declared a radical departure from the style of their contemporaries. These artists included some already mentioned above such as Jacques Adnet and René Prou, as well as Pierre Chareau, Francis Jourdain, Raymond Templier, and architects René Herbst, Robert Mallet-Stevens, André Lurcat, and others.

Le Corbusier set the philosophical tone of the Modern movement, declaring that furnishings should be made in the service of man and not art. In 1927 he designed chairs and tables of various types which were manufactured by Thonet in tubing, metal, and glass. The chair coverings were simple pieces of canvas held taut by spring fastenings. However, his best known chair uses pony skin stretched between metal tube supports.

René Herbst was one of the main designers responsible for the split with traditional French designers. He was openly hostile to all decoration, and made prolific use of metal, steel, aluminum, and other new materials. His colleague, Francis Jourdain, was determined, in a Socialistic way, to produced low-priced furniture for the masses. Décoration Interieur Moderne (DIM), founded by René Joubert in 1919, became one of the first French companies to start producing chrome furniture a few years later. In 1931, Practical Equipment Limited (PEL) opened in England, obviously influenced by the idea of furniture as "equipment." The leading designers of furniture in England were Serge Chermayeff and Welles Coates, both architects.

Works by the French Moderns have long been sought after, as they represent an innovative and pivotal point in 20th-century design. A circa-1930 aluminum desk by Herbst realized $35,250 at Christie's in 2000; a mahogany settee by Jourdain brought more than 161,000 euros in a Sotheby's Paris auction in 2003; and a single armchair by DIM was recently offered on the retail market for $12,500.

Not all Art Deco furniture in France was designer-made. There is also a great quantity of well-made furniture that I can only call "French Provincial Art Deco"—dining room sets, sideboards, and tables in oak, sycamore, and other native woods, carved with stylized fruits and flowers, and often with marble tops. Generally, this furniture uses Art Deco motifs on otherwise traditional, heavy French country furniture. Less adventurous than Parisian high-style, it can nonetheless be a good example of Art Deco, and it is generally priced at what one would pay for any other well-made, vintage furniture.

Mass-produced English wooden furniture of the 1930s also appears on the market, and the most notable examples on the market are the bar cabinets, armoires, and other furnishings designed by Ray Hille, which have become quite expensive, reaching more than $10,000 for the best examples. Incredibly restored bars and bar cabinets are a specialty at Deco-Dence in Dallas, which always has several outstanding examples on hand.

American furniture design, which had been evolving on its own in the 1920s, was much more influenced by the

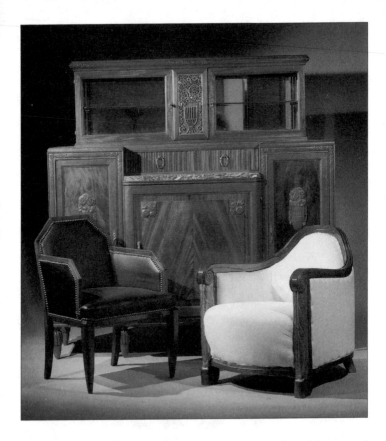

A French buffet with carved decoration, and two French armchairs, all ca. 1930. Courtesy of Ivey-Selkirk, St. Louis.

Bauhaus and the Moderns than it was by Ruhlmann and Süe et Mare. Many designers had emigrated to the United States from Austria, Germany, and Scandinavia.

The Bauhaus, founded by Walter Gropius in 1919, relocated to the United States in the 1930s. Gropius became a professor of architecture at Harvard University. Other Bauhaus designers such as Ludwig Mies van der Rohe and Marcel Breuer would also come to America. Many of their designs were originally issued (and have been extensively reissued) by Knoll International, founded in 1938, and well-known for their office furniture.

Scandinavian countries were quick to develop simplified modern design when faced with the austerity of the global Depression. Perhaps the best-known Finnish designer is Alvar Aalto, known for his streamlined designs for chairs, armchairs, and tables. Eliel Saarinen, who em-

igrated to America from Finland, became the first director of the Cranbrook Academy of Art in 1922, and influenced countless American designers. The impact of Scandivanian Modern design would be strongly felt in the late 1930s and into the 1940s in the work of Charles and Rae Eames, George Nelson, and Eero Saarinen, Eliel's son, who designed bent plywood furniture that was marketed through Knoll. Aalto's early bentwood furniture designs both presaged the Streamline phase of Art Deco and were the forerunners of the Biomorphism of the 1940s and 1950s.

Furniture by early Scandinavian designers such as Alvar Aalto is sought after as both innovative design in its own right and precedent-setting in its impact on 20th-century design. An early "Paimio" chair designed by Aalto in 1933 from laminated birch and beech realized $38,240 at Phillips, de Pury & Luxembourg in 2002. Other early chairs have sold in the $20,000-plus range at auction in recent years. However, mass-produced tables, stools,

Bar cabinet by Ray Hille in amboyna and lacquer, ca. 1935. Courtesy of Deco-Dence, TX.

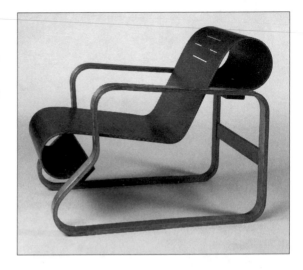

armchairs, and others designs by Aalto for Artek, can often be purchased for less than $1,000 and sometimes less than $500 at auction.

America really had no strong native style of furniture since the American Colonial style. Many movements had their heydays: Chippendale, Tudor, Victorian Gothic, Rococo, Eastlake, and Arts and Crafts among them. However, when Art Deco design reached America, the forces of the Prairie School and Frank Lloyd Wright were already at work, transforming the shape of both architecture and furnishings in America.

Another architect, Joseph Urban, who emigrated from Vienna, had a strong influence on both architecture and American decorative arts of the period. He was director of the Wiener Werkstätte Gallery in New York City, where he displayed a variety of furniture that reflected the Modernist movements of Europe.

Eugene Schoen was another early Modernist in America, establishing an architectural practice in New York City in 1905. He produced only one-of-a-kind items that have traces of both French and German influences, and his work is rare and expensive on the market. His work has been compared to Ruhlmann's, in that it is monumental, unadorned, and often relies often on the grain of the wood for its design.

Paul Frankl "Skyscraper" chest of drawers, ca. 1927, in maple, Bakelite, glass and brass. Courtesy of Phillips, de Pury & Luxembourg, NY.

Paul Frankl stands out as the first major Modernist designer in America. Born in Vienna, he studied in Berlin and Copenhagen before arriving in New York City in 1914. It was he who noted that the 1925 Exposition in Paris would have been markedly different if America had been able to display a skyscraper or two.

Skyscrapers were the inspiration for his extraordinary custom-made desks, wardrobes, and bookcases, introduced in 1926. Generally made in California redwood with nickel-plated steel or lacquered trim and interiors, these met with immediate acclaim, and can sell for tens of thousands of dollars today—if they can be found on the open market. A fine example of one of his bookcases in red and black lacquer sold at David Rago Auctions in 2001 for $37,500, and other examples can sell even higher.

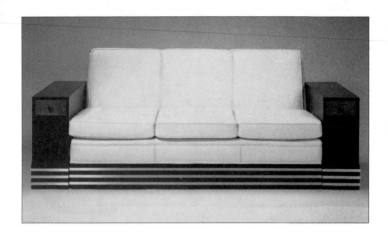

Sofa with two end tables, attributed to Paul Frankl, ca. 1930s. Courtesy of Phillips, de Pury & Luxembourg, NY.

Creations for his own firms, the Skyscraper Furniture Company, and later the Frankl Galleries, and his special commissions are the highest-priced overall. A club chair and ottoman he designed especially for the Behrendt House in Los Angeles sold for $65,725 at Phillips, de Pury & Luxembourg in 2002. A Frankl Galleries sofa with two end tables in ebonized wood, chromed metal, and white leather, sold at the same auction for $17,925. A single deep-seated Frankl "Speed Chair," part of a line he created in 1933, can bring as much as $25,000. (See Recognizing Art Deco for a photo of Frankl's "Speed Chair.")

Although some criticize Frankl's work for its use of cheaper materials and sometimes less-than-elegant finishing and enameling, his conceptual strength shows through. Frankl was also a great spokesperson for the Modern movement, and a prolific writer who spread his design ideas by example and through the written word. Later, he would contribute his talents to designs for production furniture for Johnson Furniture, Brown-Saltzman, and Barker Brothers department store in Los Angeles.

Good examples of these designs can often be purchased for less than $2,000 and sometimes for less than $1,000. While less distinctively Art Deco in design, sometimes created in the 1940s and even the early 1950s, and mass-produced in some quantity, they are still by a leading American Modernist and will no doubt appreciate in value over time. Frankl also designed a popular Modernist line of rattan furniture, and recent retail prices offered a rattan club chair at $825, a loveseat at $1,550, and a three-piece sectional sofa at $1,795.

Urban living spaces and the American lifestyle called for furniture to change dramatically once again. Built-in closets and cupboards eliminated the need for wardrobes and kitchen stands. Dining room tables were given drawers for silverware. Even baby grand pianos were designed by Chickering, Steinway, and others in the new Modern style. Fireplace chairs disappeared with fireplaces. Metal and glass increasingly replaced wood. Upholstered "easy chairs" and sofas became popular, and modular furniture could be arranged to fit smaller spaces better. With the end of Prohibition in 1933, liquor cabinets, bars, stools, and other leisure furniture proliferated. Also, a host of synthetic industrial materials came into use, known by their familiar trade names such as Formica, Bakelite, and Plexiglass.

Donald Deskey is a giant in many fields of American design. He founded his own design firm, Deskey-Vollmer, with partner Phillip Vollmer in 1927. His first furniture designs were private commissions, and he went on to design for manufacturers such as Ypsilanti Reed Furniture Company, Widdicomb, S. Karpen & Company in Chicago, and others. More than 400 pieces of his work were put into production in the five-year period of 1930–1934, and many feel his crowning achievement was the interiors and furnishings for Radio City Music Hall. A black painted chrome ash stand he designed for Radio City was offered in 2003 for $3,600.

Deskey's designs for his own company, AMODEC (American Modern Decoration), are also sought after. A 37" high sideboard in this line, introduced in 1935, was recently on the market for $4,900. A bedroom suite by Deskey for Widdicomb comprised of a tall chest, vanity and mirror, a bench, and nightstand with maple drawer fronts and mahogany tops was also being offered for $6,500. Better examples of his designs, for smaller side tables, floor lamps, and chairs often sell at auction for $2,000 or less, but ten years ago those items were often bringing less than $500.

KEM Weber armchair by Grand Rapids Chair Company, ca. 1929 in green painted wood and leather. Courtesy of Phillips, de Pury & Luxembourg, NY.

Another notable designer is Kem Weber, born Karl Emmanuel Martin Weber, in Berlin. He even streamlined his own name, taking his initials KEM as a surname. Weber went to San Francisco in 1914 to work on the German pavilion for the Panama–Pacific Exposition, and was forced to remain there when war broke out. After the war he moved to Los Angeles, became art director for Barker Brothers, and then opened his own design studio there in 1927. He was perhaps the only notable Modernist furniture designer on America's west coast, where he became friends with architect Richard Neutra. Weber also created some furniture for S. Karpen & Company, and tubular metal designs for Lloyd Manufacturing.

One of Weber's most famous Art Deco designs is his "Airline Chair," designed in 1934 for the Airline Chair Company in Los Angeles. Not intended for use on an airline, it is simply a great Streamline-style birch and ash chair that owes much to Scandinavian designers. An example of this chair sold for $7,170 at Christie's New York in 2003. An even rarer armchair from "the Kem Weber Group," manufactured by Grand Rapids Chair Company in green painted wood and original leather, sold for $17,925 at Phillips, de Pury & Luxembourg in 2002.

Other important American furniture designers include Gilbert Rohde and Wolfgang Hoffmann. Among other things, Wolfgang Hoffmann, the son of Vienna Secessionist Josef Hoffmann, designed a line of metal, enamel, and glass furniture for The Howell Company in Geneva, Illinois. These striking designs can still be acquired relatively inexpensively, probably due in part to the poor chromium plating, laminated or glass tops, and lacquer that chips easily. Some of his designs for Howell can go quite high, however, such as a Modernist rocking

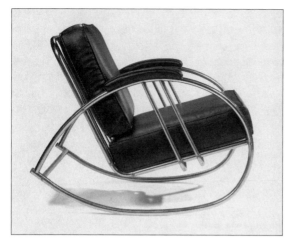

Wolfgang Hoffmann rocking chair in chromed tubular steel and leather, for the Howell Company, ca. 1930s. Courtesy of Phillips, de Pury & Luxembourg, NY.

chair which sold for more than $5,000 at auction in 2003.

In the late 1920s, Gilbert Rohde's studio furniture was already being collected by wealthy clients in New York, and his own line of production furniture was being carried by Lord & Taylor. In 1930 he became chief designer for Herman Miller, producing new lines of furniture, clocks, and lighting fixtures through 1941. The best sources for identifying these works are the original Herman Miller catalogues of the 1930s and 1940s, many of which are available today as reprints. Rohde also designed for Troy Sunshade in Ohio, Heywood-Wakefield, Kroehler Manufacturing in Chicago, and others until his untimely death in 1944.

Recent prices for Rohde material being offered on the retail market include $5,500 for a cabinet in mahogany, amboyna, and rosewood designed for Herman Miller in 1938. Another cabinet, in Paldao wood, a Philippine wood, designed in 1940 for the same company was offered at $3,900. Even a coffee table for Herman Miller was priced at $4,500. Better examples of his designs for Herman Miller can often be purchased at auction in the $2,000 to $6,000 range, although every year seems to bring increases.

Rohde's designs for Troy Sunshade can be more affordable. At a 2002 auction, two small chrome and black

Formica tables sold for $1,700, a green vinyl-topped settee and armchair for as little as $1,000. However, a Troy Sunshade chrome and black lacquered desk with a matching "Z" chair by the designer brought $4,000. And a hard-to-find 1934 armchair he created for Heywood-Wakefield (shown on the cover of this book) sold at Phillips, de Pury & Luxembourg in 2002 for $7,768.

One of the best single resources today for furniture by American Modernist designers is Ric Emmett of Modernism Gallery in Coral Gables, Florida. For almost three decades, Emmett has uncovered and documented work by Deskey, Frankl, Hoffmann, Rohde, and others, and has helped to promote these designers to their rightful place in the annals of Art Deco design.

While Walter Dorwin Teague and Norman Bel Geddes are both towering figures in American design of the era, they are perhaps best known for their industrial design. Both did some furniture design: Teague designed for S. Karpen & Company, and Bel Geddes designed one of the first lines of case metal furniture for Simmons in 1930.

Russel Wright also created a number of designs for his own "American Modern" furniture line, and for the Massachusetts manufacturer Heywood-Wakefield, for whom he created the "Flexible Modern Line." Both are good examples of the style as it evolved toward the 1940s.

At first, the industry in America was focused on wooden furniture, and centered mostly in Grand Rapids, Michigan, where it had the resources of numerous European immigrant cabinetmakers. Major manufacturers included Imperial Furniture Company, Grand Rapids Chair and Bookcase Company, among others. Grand Rapids lost its preeminent place in American furniture-making in part because it was slow to respond to the push toward production metal furniture.

There were numerous American metal furniture manufacturers in the 1930s, including those already mentioned, such as Herman Miller, Widdicomb, Troy Sunshade, Simmons, Lloyd, Mutual Sunset Company, and Royal Metal Furniture. Many of the designs of these companies look so alike that, unless there is a company

Norman Bel Geddes dressing table and mirror, 1933 for Simmons Furniture, in chromium plated steel, enamel, brass and glass. Courtesy of Phillips, de Pury & Luxembourg, NY.

mark or label, or you are armed with original catalogues, it is often hard to tell the difference.

Another notable metal furniture designer, Warren McArthur, designed for his own manufacturing company in New York City, which used spun aluminum extensively in furniture.

McArthur's furniture designs are now highly sought after. The flexibility and strength of spun aluminum allowed the creation of unique designs for lounge chairs, settees, armchairs, and more. The other advantage of spun aluminum is that it is more durable than chrome (which pits and rusts), increasing the chances of finding this furniture in excellent condition.

Auction prices keep going up on this production: a rare McArthur lounge chair and ottoman from the Arizona Biltmore Hotel sold for $5,500 in 2000 at David Rago Auctions, and a library desk in aluminum and black Formica by the designer sold for $29,900 at Phillips, de Pury & Luxembourg in 2002.

An unusual Warren McArthur tete-a-tete in machined aluminum, leatherette cushions and rubber feet. Courtesy of Century Design, Ltd., MO.

The least expensive American Art Deco furniture is the overstuffed mohair furniture that was popular during the Depression. Today, this furniture is being refinished and reupholstered, and many people find it stylish, functional, comfortable, and durable—the very reasons it was popular in the 1930s. Where the influence of Art Deco can really be seen is in the lines of the chairs and sofas that are so futuristically exaggerated that they have been called "Buck Rogers thrones."

Metalware

In metalware, there is no question that the dominant artist of early Art Deco is Edgar Brandt. Brandt's work is remarkable for the combination of traditional skills and the use of new technology. Autogenous welding, a process that permits two different metals to be welded together, and the new power hammer, were used by him. The use of these tools also allowed for greater production and lower costs. Today his gates, lamps, andirons, wrought-iron mounted tables, fire screens, and other works are very expensive, and one of his monumental screens called "L'Oasis" is tied for the world record for

Machine Age andirons, ca. 1930s, in solid brass. Courtesy of Century Design, Ltd., MO.

an Art Deco object at auction, bringing $1,876,000 in 2000 at Christie's New York. (See Today's Market for more information.)

In 1926 Brandt did the metal work for the Cheney building in New York City, and opened a branch of his company there, with the result that some major Brandt material has surfaced over the years in the United States. Other French designers who are sought after for their work in metal include Raymond Subes, Paul Kiss, and Nic Frères.

Known for his metalwork in a more traditional way was sculptor William Hunt Diederich. Born in Hungary in 1884, Diederich emigrated to America like so many of his contemporaries. He worked primarily on Long Island, and died in 1953. Diederich was noted for weathervanes, fireplace screens, and other metalwork.

Metalwares such as andirons by Donald Deskey and Russel Wright also command attention and can bring high prices on the market. For example, a pair of 1930 Russel Wright "Fire Deer" andirons sold for $12,650 at auction in 2002. Many striking, better examples of Modernist designs for andirons and fireplace screens are still available, although prices have risen as their popularity has increased in recent years. One of the best resources we have identified for these is Century Design, Ltd. In St. Louis.

French wrought iron hall tree and umbrella stand, ca. 1930s. Courtesy of First 1/2, CA.

The metalwork of Oscar B. Bach, who emigrated to New York from Germany, is increasingly drawing attention on the market; in particular, his designs for mirrors, lighting, and other furnishings. Bach did the metalwork on the Empire State Building and for the interiors of the Chrysler Building and Radio City Music Hall. Not all of Bach's sometimes overly ornamental work can properly be called "Art Deco," but that alone won't prevent it from having an increased following in the years ahead.

Some striking Art Deco designs for household furnishings in wrought iron can still be affordably acquired, such as hall racks, coat racks, consoles, and hanging mirrors. Anonymously designed, fairly large quantities of these were produced in the Art Deco style to furnish middle-class apartments in Paris, and have become real specialties for a few dealers in the United States, such as Jacques Caussin of First 1/2 in Palm Springs. These items have the same high-style appearance as wrought iron by Brandt, Kiss, and others, but at a fraction of the cost.

Lighting and Lamps

One of the leading figures of early Art Deco design for lighting is Albert Cheuret, whose works are very expensive and who often used alabaster for the shades. A recent retail offering on a Cheuret 15" table lamp in silvered bronze with an alabaster shade was $18,500.

Many noted lamp designers were glassmakers, such as René Lalique, Daum Nancy, Charles Schneider, and Degué. Sought-after today for their finely-designed and still affordable chandeliers is the French firm Muller Frères. While a Lalique chandelier can easily cost $20,000, one can still find a better Muller Frères frosted

An elegant Meuller Freres chandelier, ca. 1925, in nickel over bronze with in frosted glass shades. Courtesy of Moderne, PA.

glass chandelier in the range of $3,000 to $5,000, and better table lamps often in the $2,000 to $3,000 range.

Several of the metal designers named above also designed lighting fixtures incorporating metal. Edgar Brandt worked with Daum to create luxurious table lamps and *torchères*, literally "torches," or floor lamps. Today, they are sought after by glass collectors as well as by Brandt collectors, and can be very expensive.

Figural and sculptural lamps also increased in popularity. Another noted artist was Jean Goulden, who was influenced by Byzantine enameling and created visually appealing geometric and abstract designs for lamps, as well as other furnishings. Jean Perzel, a Czechoslovakian who emigrated to France, also created fine designs for lighting.

Collectors should take note of the many wonderful, anonymous designs for chandeliers and other lighting fixtures produced in a French style in the United States in the

1920s. Created by such companies as Lincoln, Lightolier and Markel, they were often produced in painted or patinated cast base metals instead of wrought iron, but are well-designed and affordable. Both Consolidated Lamp and Glass and Phoenix Glass also produced chandeliers and wall sconces which can still easily be found.

Lorial and Bryan Francis of decodame.com in Naples, Florida, and Jack Beeler at Decorum in San Francisco are two excellent sources for Art Deco lighting and lamps.

Perhaps the best-known American lighting designer is Walter von Nessen. After studying in Berlin under the progressive architect Bruno Paul, he settled in New York City in 1925, and opened his own studio two years later. He received commissions for architectural lighting, as well as doors, vestibules, and elevator cabs.

While he is also known for his houseware designs for Chase Brass and Copper, as well as for small metal furnishings, he is most highly regarded for his design of lamps, using chrome, aluminum, glass, Bakelite, and other modern materials. Nessen Lighting continues to manufacture many of his innovative swing-arm designs today.

Many have wrongly attributed the outstanding design of the Pattyn Lamp featured on our cover to von Nessen. In fact, these futuristic lamps were designed by Pierre Pat-

The evolution of Art Deco: A French Meuller Freres table lamp in wrought iron, ca. 1925; a skyscraper-inspired Salterini "Tabletop Torchere" in bronze, ca. 1928; and a Streamlined table lamp in chromium plate and Bakelite, ca. 1930s. Author's collection. Photo by Robert Four.

tyn, founder of the Detroit-based Modern Products Corporation, and some styles were produced into the early 1950s. Eric Menard and Peter Linden of Decodence in San Francisco have developed a specialty for Pattyn lamps and did considerable digging before finding advertisements for some styles in *House Beautiful* magazine for May and June, 1950. Advertised at $23.75 and $31.50, these lamps now sell for $4,000 to $5,000, with rare designs that have three-way push buttons in Lucite bringing as much as $7,500.

Other residential and commercial lamp designers of the day include Donald Deskey, Walter Dorwin Teague, Kem Weber for Miller Lamp Company, Gilbert Rohde, Kurt Versen for Lightolier, and Carl Sorensen. Through the 1920s and 1930s, dozens of companies produced decorative and commercial lighting fixtures. A new term, "illuminating engineers," came into being, and many unique designs were created.

An early American Modernist lighting designer whose work rarely appears on the market is John B. Salterini,

French clock, signed P. Fargette, ca. 1925, in silver, copper and gilt brass, with an onyx face and base. Courtesy of *decodame. com*, FL.

who went on to design wrought iron furniture into the 1940s and early 1950s. Salterini's wrought iron studio was on West 23rd Street in New York in the 1920s. About the same time Frankl was creating Skyscraper Furniture, Salterini was creating stepped-back angular "Tabletop Torchères" and angular lamps in iron and frosted glass.

Happily for collectors, many styles of Machine Age table and floor lamps are available in chrome, Bakelite, spun aluminum, and other materials for $200 to $500, with better examples still less than $1,000.

Clocks

No pun intended, but one can watch the evolution of the Art Deco style ticking away in the design of the clocks that were always a part of furnishing a household, from key-wound mantel and wall clocks, to battery-operated clocks, to streamlined digital electric models.

In the early Art Deco period, French clocks were often made of gilt wood or bronze and marble, and designed with fruit, flowers, and stylized birds or nudes. Süe et Mare were known for their high-style French Art Deco mantel clocks. Albert Guenot also created clocks in gilt wood, and a stunning example was offered on the market recently at $6,800. Albert Cheuret, mentioned above for his lighting designs, was also an outstanding designer of clocks. Luxurious glass clocks were made by Lalique, fabulous jeweled bedside and mantel clocks were made by Cartier, and silver designer Jean Puiforcat contributed some stunning designs.

French ceramic mantel clock, signed D'Argyl, ca. 1930. Author's collection. Photo by Robert Four.

In France in the 1920s and 1930s, many manufacturers produced mantel clocks with *garniture*. Literally translated as "garnish," these were two additional pieces placed on either side of the central clock to decorate the mantel. Clock garnitures had been made previously, but the Deco style made use of marble or onyx set in geometric patterns. In addition, the clock itself may be surmounted with bronze or brass figures. Some had figures of Amazons or distinctively styled animals. These Art Deco mantel clocks still remain fairly affordable, with a good set often selling in the $500–$1,000 range.

One of the earliest patents for battery-operated clocks was held by Léon Hatot, who named his company ATO.

ATO movements were used by many manufacturers including Elgin, Seth Thomas, and Bulova, so collectors see the name often. You'll find some good and better examples of Art Deco clocks in the market with the name ATO on the face, many at very affordable prices.

American manufacturers of clocks that are sought after today are Herman Miller, Pennwood Numechron, Seth Thomas, J. E. Caldwell, and Manning Bowman, which still produced clocks in wood and/or marble before switching to chrome. Pennwood started making clocks in the mid-

"Modernique," 1928, by Paul Frankl for Telechron. Courtesy of Bonhams and Butterfields, CA.

1930s and created a series of early digital designs they dubbed "Numechrons." Again, this is an area where you can find good and better examples of Art Deco design still selling for $200 to $500.

Paul Frankl's only design of a clock for Telechron has also become something of an icon, the #431 "Modernique" in 1928, which launched a whole new era in Art Deco clock design with its sunburst face and stepped-back case. An example of this clock sold at a Wright auction in 2003 for $1,200, a price which has held steady over several years.

The same auction saw a streamlined digital Kem Weber clock bring $2,300. Weber's digital clock designs for Lawson Time, Inc., such as his "Zephyr" clock, are among the most notable of the era, streamlined in design, though not any more in price.

Gilbert Rohde created several clock designs for Herman Miller, which are now sought-after icons of American design, especially his "Z" clock, a mint example of which sold for $5,000 at David Rago Auctions in 2001, and might bring much more today, as it was one of the items featured in the museum exhibition "American Modern 1925–1940: Design for a New Age," organized by the

Metropolitan Museum of Art, which traveled through July 2002. Drawn from the outstanding collection of John C. Waddell, the exhibition and the accompanying book again fired up the collecting world for American Modernism. ◙

7

DECORATIVE SCULPTURE

In Europe especially, the Art Deco era saw a closer *rapprochement*, or coming together, of the fine arts and the decorative arts than ever before. Fine artists were commissioned to create designs for the applied arts, and designers borrowed concepts and innovations of form from the world of fine arts. In consequence, or as part of that process, decorative sculpture came more into demand, building on a popularity that had started in the Art Nouveau period.

In sculpture, as in certain other areas, such as works on paper, it is sometimes difficult (and sometimes arbitrary) to delineate between what is "decorative art" and what is "fine art." In the world of Art Deco, this confusion has been further caused by the misuse of the terminology.

Perhaps the best way of distinguishing decorative sculpture from fine art sculpture is the *intent* behind its creation. Decorative sculpture was commissioned expressly for commercial production and distribution. Its goal was not necessarily to break new ground in an artistic way, but rather to be visually appealing, even purposefully beautiful, in order to function as a decorative component in interior design. However, the often breathtaking qualities of decorative sculpture have led to the use of the term "decorative works of art," which seems to bridge the gap. Prices bridged the gap years ago, and some "decorative" sculpture now commands higher prices than its "fine art" counterpart.

Happily, in the Art Deco period, advances in bronze casting made it possible to more easily produce and distribute statues to satisfy the new markets. Many artists, such as Belgian Claire Jeanne Roberte Colinet, began in the tradition of fine arts and were later commissioned for works that would be produced in larger quantities.

Underscoring the commercial intent of the manufacturers who produced them, in addition to larger quantities and recastings as the market grew, many of these works were also produced in different sizes. Some were mounted on bases, and others on trays. The higher-priced models might be mounted on marble, and the lower-priced ones on quartz.

Where fine artists most often did not paint the bronze beyond overall patination in green, brown, or black, many of the new decorative statues were polychromed in bright colors and mounted on bases of colorful marble or onyx.

After World War I, decorative bronze sculptures were produced for and distributed through major department stores. For example, Pomone at Au Bon Marché commissioned artists to create works specifically for their stores. Many were sold through the Phillips & MacConnal Gallery in London. In addition to larger decorative sculpture, Marcel Bouraine created cast bronze bookends, decorative ashtrays, and paperweights designed as stylized small animals, which were distributed through Alfred Dunhill in New York.

Art Deco sculpture reflected the new design style with lithe nude and semi-nude maidens, most often dancing, and sometimes flying through the sky. The female figure—real, mythical, or exotic—was the most popular subject for decorative statues. Often the subject was a well-known singer, actress, or personality, such as Josephine Baker or Nijinski. The costumes and cultures of India, Egyptian, Africa, Persia, and other "exotic" lands were also favorite subjects.

Sporting figures, again often of women, also became popular: archers, tennis players, golfers, swimmers, fencers, and javelin throwers. Other sculptures were cast as figures of children, jesters, school masters, and other "characters."

Not far behind women in popularity was the *animalier* movement in modern sculpture. No longer restrained by the Beaux Arts tradition of realistic portrayal of animals, the Art Deco period elongated, streamlined and otherwise "tamed" wild beasts, into the modern idiom.

Gone were the wild boars ferociously attacking a stallion. In their place appeared greyhounds, gazelles, and the large cats, perfect subjects for the sleek new look. Edouard Marcel Sandoz was noted for his sculptures of animals, and François Pompon is one of the best known artists of the modern *animalier* movement. In 1922 at the Salon d'Automne in Paris, he exhibited a marble statue of a polar bear which is credited with starting the modern depiction of animals using smooth lines and frozen poses.

Chryselephantine Statues

By far the most popular—and most expensive—statues of the Art Deco era are "chryselephantine," or bronze and ivory. Popular for at least two decades before the Art Deco period, they reached their peak of production during the late 1920s until the mid-1930s.

The term "chryselephantine" was first used to describe the statues that used both gold and ivory in ancient Greece. During the Art Nouveau era, the Belgians, the most prolific producers of bronze and ivory statues, extended the meaning to encompass any statue fashioned in combination with ivory.

Ivory has always held the interest of sculptors for its beauty and ease of carving. Ivory also ages and yellows in attractive ways. In the middle of the 19th century, however, ivory was being used primarily for everyday items like brushes and door handles.

When the Congo was conquered by the Belgians, ivory tusks were shipped back to Europe in quantities that far exceeded household uses, and which would enrage conservationists today. In 1894, the Secretary of State for the Congo Free State called on Belgian artists to use more ivory, and it was further officially encouraged by commissions and competition exhibitions.

However, the basic materials that were used—bronze, ivory and marble—would change as the market for the statues grew. Cheaper metals, such as spelter, a type of zinc which is more akin to pewter and molds more easily, would come into use for less expensive statues. A plastic composition, called "ivorene," which only sometimes actually contains a small amount of powdered ivory, replaced the real thing.

The bases, which at first were made of high-quality marble and even lapis lazuli, and which had increased the status of the statues as precious objets, changed to cheaper marble and finally seamed onyx or other marble-like stones. The best onyx came from Brazil, and was a favorite material for other decorative objects as well.

These statues, along with many decorative bronze-only pieces, were ignored for many years, but there was a strong resurgence of interest in the early to mid-1970s. At that time, leading scholars and dealers, such as Brian Catley, Victor Arwas and Alain Lesieutre would reawaken the collecting market's interest in them.

Prices rose dramatically until about 1983 when a flood of reproductions, created both in the United States and abroad, hit the market, setting back prices considerably. Since then, prices have not only recovered, but have risen higher than ever. However, the reproductions are still a scourge, and unwary collectors get taken every day. Bronze-only statues have also been reproduced in quantity. Because most of these statues are not protected by copyright, a manufacturer can simply cast a mold from one and start production. (For more information on sculpture reproductions, please see the Fakes Alert! chapter.)

The reproductions are often sold for a few hundred dollars to a thousand dollars. Authentic castings of bronze and ivory figures command thousands of dollars, or even tens of thousands of dollars in today's Art Deco market, depending on the design, the size, materials used, the artist, the subject, and the workmanship. Price alone is not the best indicator to use in discerning a fake, as a fake can also be sold with a high price tag.

The best auction houses and dealers use standardized language to indicate the casting of statues. When a bronze is made from the artist's original model and was cast during the artist's lifetime or shortly thereafter, they will describe it as "Cast *from* a model" by the artist. When it is a later casting, they will describe it as "Cast *after* a model" by the artist. If the seller you are speaking with does not make this distinction, the best advice is to move on.

French Sculpture

In Paris, the firm Etling, known to many for their frosted Lalique-like glass, was the largest *editeur* of decorative sculpture, employing artists such as Colinet, Demetre H. Chiparus, Jean Descomps, Maurice Guiraud-Rivière, Marcel Bouraine and others. The Goldscheider firm in Paris was also a large manufacturer, and issued works by artists such as Alexander Kelety, Pierre Traverse, and Pierre Le Faguays.

Demetre H. Chiparus leads the market as the foremost name in decorative sculpture of the period (and is the most often forged as well). Chiparus came to study in Paris from his native Romania, and exhibited at the Salon des Artistes Français from 1914 to 1918. He is best known for his bronze and ivory figures of exotic dancers, with subjects often taken from the contemporary performing arts, such as his "Russian Dancers," identified as Nijinski and Ida Rubenstein of the Ballets Russes.

Chiparus is best known for the spectacular design and elaborate treatment and patination of the costumes his figures wore.

Chiparus's early figures, on relatively simple bases, were primarily cast by Etling. Later pieces were made by the LN & JL foundry which appears to have specialized in making the more elaborate and zig-zagged marble and onyx bases.

Recent auction high points include a price realized of $101,375 for his bronze and ivory sculpture "Antinea" at Sotheby's New York in 2000, and $138,000 for his bronze and ivory "Miss Kita" at Christie's New York in

"Starlight," ca. 1925, a bronze and ivory sculpture by Demetre H. Chiparus. Courtesy of Bonhams and Butterfields, CA.

2001. In the last five years, more than fifteen works by Chiparus have sold above $20,000 at auction in New York and twice that number have sold for $10,000 or more. Recent retail listings for "Footsteps" and "Dancer of Palmyra" bronze and ivory pieces, both around 17" high, were in the range of $25,000.

The best resource on Chiparus is former New York dealer Alberto Shayo's 1999 book, *Chiparus: Master of Art Deco*. Chiparus's other figures, though not as "Deco," also include adorable children and little clowns. Claire Jeanne Roberte Colinet also worked in bronze and ivory. A native Belgian, she moved to Paris and was elected to the Société des Artistes Français in 1913. Later, she would exhibit at the Salon des Indépendants from 1937 to 1940.

Maurice Guiraud-Rivière was also a prolific sculptor, contributing models of dancers in a variety of materials to Etling, as well as models for porcelain figures to Sèvres and Robj. Guiraud-Rivière is also known for subjects relating to speed, such as motor car racing, charioteering, and steeple chasing, which allowed him to significantly utilize horizontal styling. One of his most outstanding works is an allegorical figure of a woman called "The Comet," streaking down from the sky, her hair trailing behind. A recent retail listing offered this sculpture at just over $37,000.

Apart from the bronze figures of animals for bookends and paperweights already mentioned, Marcel Bouraine is perhaps best known for his figures of battling Amazon women, which appear to have been produced in a series. Alexander Kelety, a Hungarian who came to live and work in France, was another outstanding artist of the period, working more in bronze than in bronze and ivory. A silvered bronze group of flamingoes by Kelety standing 13" high was recently on the market for only about $12,000, but a formidable example of his work entitled "The Archer" sold at Christie's New York in 2003 for $186,700.

In the 1920s, another noted French artist, Pierre Le Faguays, would also exhibit his work there. Le Faguays is best known for his lithe nude dancers, archers, and other figures of women in bronze. Le Faguays also designed models for the shop of sculptor Max Le Verrier.

Le Verrier specialized in statues, figural lamps, bookends, and other decorative, functional sculpture, often cast in cheaper metals. He created his own pieces, and also commissioned Le Faguays and other artists such as Raymond Guerbe, Fayral, and Bouraine. Le Verrier's production, and the artists associated with him, were probably the inspiration for Frankart, the American manufacturer of inexpensive sculptural bookends, lamps, ashtrays and other objects in the 1920s.

In spite of the record prices for certain artists and especially for bronze and ivory statues, good and better examples of original French Art Deco bronzes can still be purchased broadly in the range of $2,000 to $5,000. These may not have the elaborate bases or polychromed colors of the more expensive works, but they are still visually striking, and convey the essence of the Art Deco spirit.

"Message of Love," ca. 1920s, by Pierre Le Faguays. Author's collection. Photo by Robert Four.

German Sculpture

In 1906, the ivory carver Ferdinand Preiss with his partner Arthur Kassler started the firm Preiss-Kassler in Berlin, and soon came to control the market for bronze and ivory sculpture in Germany.

Preiss was, and is, as popular as Chiparus, and his work was widely distributed by the Phillips & MacConnal Gallery of Arts in London, as well as others. He created ivory-only sculptures as well as bronze and ivory, and made his reputation on the finesse with which he carved the ivory. He is perhaps best known for his sportily clad men and women, which really mirrored modern life. He also often used a cooler metallic color palette of blues, silvers, and grays.

He too created figures from the world of entertainment, such as Brigitte Helm as the human heroine of Fritz Lang's *Metropolis* and his "Bat Dancer" from the Hollywood film *Flying Down to Rio*.

Preiss commissioned other sculptors to create for his firm, such as Otto Poertzel and Paul Phillipe. The Preiss-Kassler "PK" monogram within a circle is often found stamped on the bronze portion of these statues.

"Professor Poertzel," as he was called, created bronze and ivory sculptures of cabaret and burlesque performers and circus stars. Phillipe's chryselephantines are usually women with elongated bodies and sharply pointed features. He designed several statues in ivory only, as did Preiss, and these tend to be far less expensive than the chryselephantine sculptures.

Viennese Sculpture
In Vienna, the firm of Frederich Goldscheider manufactured bronze and ivory sculpture, mostly by Joseph Lorenzl. Lorenzl's figures of dancers and fashionable women are very stylized, and were also produced in ivory alone or in spelter. Decorative bronzes were also made by the Bergman and Argentor foundries in Vienna, the latter issuing several works by Bruno Zach.

Zach was also commissioned by Preiss, but worked mainly in Austria, and is best known for his erotic sculptures in bronze and ivory. He often depicted his women in leather trousers, smoking cigarettes, or wearing garters. Zach also designed a few bronzes with "exotic" American Western themes—cowboys and Indians on horseback, sleekly galloping across plains he had never seen.

With its emphasis on functionality, the Vienna Secession did not produce many decorative sculptures for their own sake. However, one Austrian name does stand out on the collecting market: Atelier Hagenauer. Sculptures by this workshop, mostly from the late 1920s and early 1930s, were often retailed through department stores and at times were commissioned by the Wiener Werkstätte.

Franz Hagenauer used a wide variety of materials to fashion his work, including chromed metal, wood, silver, nickel, brass, and painted bronze. In recent years, his work has seen greatly renewed interest on the Art Deco market. Some interesting design comparisons can be made to his work and the figural bookends and other pieces designed by Walter von Nessen and other designers for Chase Brass and Copper.

His work ranges from 24" high chromed metal busts to knick-knack sized animals to life-size figures of jazz musicians. Prices for Hagenauer also range widely. Recent auction prices range from $6,000 for a 21" high polished chromed sculpture of a woman's head to $1,200 for a pair of andirons in the form of an African man and woman, to smaller pieces that sold for less than $300, such as a 4 1/2" figure of a skier on a slope. However, ex-

A bronze and ivory sculpture of an Amazon on horseback by Bruno Zach, Austrian, ca. 1930. Author file photo.

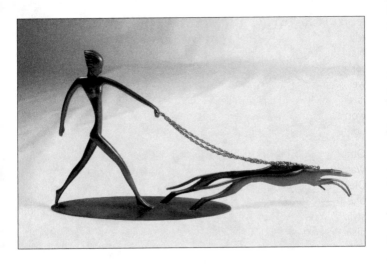

Bronze sculpture of a woman walking two greyhounds, ca. 1930, by Hagenauer. Courtesy of Century Design, Ltd., MO.

ceptional works by Hagenauer can now bring $20,000 and more.

Fine Art Sculpture

Both fine art and monumental sculpture attracted numerous talented artists in the Art Deco era, both in Europe and America. Affected by the same forces that shook the world of painting—Cubism, Fauvism, and Futurism—sculpture took on new form.

In Europe, artists working in several media, such as Alexander Archipenko, Gustav Miklos, and Josef Csaky, a Hungarian who worked in France, would translate into sculpture the new dimensions that Cubists were reflecting on the two-dimensional plane. Early fine sculpture of the period was also inspired by African masks and motifs from other ancient cultures as the Western world opened up to new influences.

Today the work of these artists is represented in "fine art," as opposed to "decorative art" auctions. Many of the sculptures created by these artists were produced in very small editions; thus, prices are correspondingly high. For example, Archipenko made bronzes usually in editions of no more than twelve, and Miklos sometimes made editions as small as four.

In America, fine sculptural artists include many who were commissioned for public monuments and architectural sculpture. Distinguished sculptors include Paul Manship, Anna Hyatt Huntington, Carl Milles, Elie Nadelman, Carl Paul Jennewein, and architectural sculptor Lee Lawrie, whose "Atlas" at Rockefeller Center is well-known. Manship's "Prometheus," created in 1934, is another famous Rockefeller Center sculpture. Some works by Manship now sell for close to $1 million at auction, and several reach the range of $250,000 or more.

Other notable American sculptors include Sydney Waugh, the avant-garde John Storrs, William Hunt Diederich, and Waylande Gregory. Boris Lovet-Lorski, one of the most outstanding sculptors working in a very stylized Art Deco manner, came to America briefly from his native Lithuania before finally settling in France.

Some of these artists are known to collectors of other Art Deco items: Waylande Gregory designed ceramics pieces for Cowan Pottery; Diederich created metalware such as weathervanes and fireplace screens; Lovet-Lorski also created fine lithographic prints; and Waugh designed glass for Steuben.

In 2003 at auction in New York, a William Hunt Diederich sculpture called "The Jockey" set a new record for the artist, bringing $19,800 for the 17" bronze. Lovet-Lorski is also known for his sculpture of horses, and a 19" bronze stallion by him sold for $36,000 at Sotheby's in 2003. His sculpture in marble is equally sought after. John Storrs's striking sculptures easily sell for more than $30,000 at auction, and one recently sold for just over $220,000 at Sotheby's New York.

American Decorative Sculpture

Roman Bronze Works and Gorham Foundry were the foremost bronze foundries in America, and executed both fine art and monumental sculptures for many leading artists, including some named above. In many ways they helped put the bronze sculptures of America on a par with those of Paris and Rome. They had the ability to cast very large garden statuary in bronze for the country estates of wealthy families such as the Whitneys and the Vanderbilts, and often produced pieces based on mythological subjects treated in a modernist fashion.

Several sculptors, many of them women, distinguished themselves through their work for this kind of garden sculpture: Harriet Whitney Frishmuth, Edith Parson, Janet Scudder, Malvina Hoffman, Eugenie Schonnard, and others.

Models by some of these and other artists were reduced in size for commercial distribution. Gorham Foundry had its own store in New York, and other works were sold through the Grand Central Art Gallery and Tiffany & Company.

Among the most sought after on the market today is Harriet Frishmuth, who created numerous bronze statues, and even an electroplated bronze radiator car mascot of a nude woman. A 67" original edition of her 1925–1926 sculpture "Crest of the Wave" sold at Christie's in 2001 for $82,500. The smaller 21" version issued by Gorham Company, which brought $8,000 to $9,000 in the early 1990s, now realizes more than $20,000 at auction, as does Anna Hyatt Huntington's well-known "Yawning Tiger" bronze, also issued by Gorham.

Frankart

Generally easy to identify, Frankart was everyman's Art Deco statuette, and plainly molded its name and usually a patent number, or "Pat. Pending" or "Pat. Appld. For," into each piece. Sometimes pieces are also dated, and a reprinting of a major Frankart Catalogue in 1981 gave serious collectors a better guide than ever before.

Collectors today should be aware, however, that the patents on several Frankart statues, ash stands and lamps, have been bought by contemporary manufacturers and are being reissued in some quantity. If the pieces are not impressed with the name of the new firm, it is up to scrupulous sellers to at least leave the tag from the current manufacturer on the piece.

Good-quality Frankart statues are real Art Deco beauties, and pioneer collectors have been gathering them up for years. However, the market for Frankart overall has been weakened by the imitations.

Frankart was art and functionality combined. Few except the earliest pieces are purely decorative. Bookends, ash stands, ashtray holders, vase stands and lamps, were the basis of Frankart's widespread popularity in this country. It was inexpensive art for everyday use.

Some of the pieces produced by the Frankart company in New York City are quite stunning. "The Spirit of Modernism" lamp, for example, had a parchment shade. For the base, abstract, tall, rectangular shapes suggested skyscrapers with irregular towers, or a cluster of skyscrapers as a city unto itself, culminating in the figure of a slender muse. This piece rarely appears on the market, and it seems that fewer of these were produced than most other Frankart lamps.

As far as is known, Frankart's first figure was introduced in 1921. It was a sleek, figural, nude candle holder, appropriately called "Flame" which had a somewhat Art Nouveau base. In the years following its immediate success, more than 100 other pieces were sculpted by the chief designer Arthur von Frankenberg. In 1923 stepped or pyramidal bases were introduced, perhaps influenced by the discovery of the tomb of Egyptian pharaoh Tutankhamen. The skyscraper style would be used not only on bases, but also on glass lamps.

Von Frankenberg did not design elaborate costumes or headdresses for his sculptures, which were usually nude women. In this way, his work often looks very similar to that of Lorenzl. Early Frankart lamps also resemble works by Max Le Verrier's company in Paris.

Frankart copyrighted its designs, but competing firms still copied them, changing only minor details. The imitators also relied on the popular nude and often green-painted women, which were thus nicknamed "greenies." The companies Nu-art and Eckart produced designs of poorer quality, which can still be found at Deco shows.

The most popular Frankart items today are still the lithe nude lamps and ash stands. However, Frankart also issued a bucking donkey lamp and bookends shaped like Scotties and bears, and these bring lower prices on both the auction and retail market.

Auction prices for Frankart pieces tend to fall mostly under $1,000 and many under $500. Better pieces, such as figural lamps, can bring more than $2,000 at auction.

After about ten years of production, the company closed its doors, one of the many Deco victims of the Depression. In the mid-1940s, most of the original molds were hauled out of storage and melted down as scrap. In theory, the numbers of good Frankart pieces are therefore somewhat limited, and there is a broad enough market among non-collectors to support good retail prices.

The collecting market situation may change in the years ahead, but one company, which owns many of the Frankart patents, has plans to continue issuing them. Because in some cases the company can work from original molds, it is hard to tell the difference. The makers of Frankart reproductions feel that they are serving a lower-end market that enjoys the Deco style but cannot afford the originals. Ironically, this was exactly Frankart's own appeal in its day. ◼

Frankart floor ashtray with ceramic insert, ca. 1935. Author's collection. Photo by Robert Four.

8
SILVER, CHROME, AND COCKTAILS

Silver

Silver underwent the same transformation of design from Art Nouveau to Art Deco as other decorative arts. However, silver continued to be produced in traditional styles as well. Long-established French companies such as Puiforcat, Tetard Frères, and Christofle produced some outstanding Art Deco designs. While their styles and lines changed, and new materials were introduced, such as ivory, wood, and semi-precious stone for handles, silver still retained its elegance.

The best designers in France were Jean Puiforcat and Jean Tetard, both of whom designed for their family firms. La Maison Desny also created some very sought-after Cubist-inspired designs in silver and silver plate. British designers who made their mark in silver included Charles Boynton and Harold Stabler. However, perhaps the best-known fine silver firm represented broadly on the Art Deco market today is Danish: Georg Jensen.

Jensen had a strong ability to create subtle Modern and Deco decorations in silver. Under his direction, talented designers such as Sigvard Bernadott, creator of the "Bernadotte" pattern, and Harald Nielsen, creator of "Pyramid" and other patterns, would bring silver into the Modern age. Some of these patterns are still in production today. Jensen's goal, which he achieved through hand-hammering and other crafts-based techniques, was to revive the art of silversmithy, which was slowly giving way to mass production. Again, not all Jensen silver can be called Art Deco, but the firm's Art Deco patterns and pieces are certainly most in demand, especially those produced before World War II. For example, a four-piece sterling silver tea set with ebony handles on an oval two-handled tray in the Pyramid pattern by Nielsen has a recent retail asking price of $45,000.

Americans were even less ready to accept new forms in silver than their French counterparts. Although they were aware of the new designs in silver, displayed as early as 1922 in the Wiener Werkstätte Gallery in New York, then under the direction of Joseph Urban, the new style had a harder time breaking ground with those who looked to Tiffany & Company as *the* silver maker of the day. Tiffany's Art Nouveau design, as well as more traditional designs from the company, had established a strong market for itself among the privileged classes, and was a deterrent to the introduction of new design.

Some of the Tiffany styles may be called Deco or Modern in inspiration, but for the most part it appears that Tiffany was making no more than a weak gesture toward the new style in designs such as "Hampton." It was not until the New York World's Fair of 1939, and just a few years prior, that Tiffany would create Modernist designs to compete with the companies that were nipping at its heels as the leading manufacturer of silver in this country.

These other manufacturers engaged leading Modern designers to create silver that would appeal to the new age.

Notable designs were produced by Eliel Saarinen, Danish-born Erik Magnussen, and German-born Peter Muller-Munk, and Walter von Nessen.

Magnussen designed for the Gorham Manufacturing of Rhode Island, which would emerge as a leader in silver design. One of his most intriguing designs is "The Lights and Shadows of Manhattan," a coffee service that used burnished silver with gold and oxidized gray panels in an asymmetrical, angular style. Look for candy dishes, serving trays, and other Magnussen designs in Gorham Silver, marked with an angular monogram "EM."

Peter Muller-Munk's 1935 "Normandie" water pitcher for Revere in chromium plated brass. Courtesy of Phillips, de Pury & Luxembourg, NY.

Peter Muller-Munk's 1935 "Normandie" water pitcher for Revere Copper and Brass has become an Art Deco icon, echoing the streamlined shape of the famous ocean liner. An example of this pitcher sold at auction for $3,500 in 2001, and we've recently seen two retail listings in about the same range.

Kem Weber designed for Porter Blanchard Silver as well as others, and his work sometimes surfaces on the market. Two other designers who have been "rediscovered" are Louis W. Rice, for Bernard Rice's Sons "Apollo Sky-Scraper" line in 1928 and Elwood N. Cornell's designs for Middletown Silverware. One Cornell coffee set sold for $8,365 in 2002 at Phillips, de Pury & Luxembourg. Other companies producing some work in the Modern idiom included International Silver, Reed & Barton, Towle Sterling, and Wilcox Silver Plate.

The Dallas Museum of Art undoubtedly has the finest collection of American Modernist silver anywhere today. In 2002, adding to its own extensive collection, it acquired the Jewel Stern Collection, the most important private collection of American silver from 1925 to 2000. Designers in the Stern Collection include Magnussen, Saarinen, and numerous less–well-known but talented industrial designers such as Belle Kogan and Elsa Tennhardt.

Elsa Tennhardt, "Cocktail Set", ca. 1928, in silver plate and glass. Courtesy of Historical Design Collection, NY.

The museum is organizing a major exhibition, "Modernism in American Silver: Design 1925–2000," which will begin a national tour in Dallas in 2005. A previous major traveling exhibition by the museum, "Silver in America, 1840–1940: A Century of Splendor," also resulted in a book by the same name, which is an excellent resource.

Under the influence of Modernism, in some cases flatware became elongated and used vertical banding to emphasize the new look. Handles and finials took on new designs, such as stepped-back skyscraper patterns that were popular for a brief period of time. Many of these companies returned to creating traditional styles after the Modernist period but, because of the Depression, their markets had dwindled.

During this time, however, a host of other companies both French and American had begun issuing sophisticated Modern designs in silver plate, which was more affordable to the general population, and which ate away at the market for sterling.

Chrome and Other Metals

Ultimately, however, companies like Revere Copper and Brass and Chase Brass and Copper Company would take up chromium and other metals for their housewares in

Elwood N. Cornell silver-plated coffee service, ca. 1928, for Middletown Silverware. Courtesy of Phillips, de Pury & Luxembourg, NY.

order to compete in the market. Chrome, nickel, and other cheap metals could be fashioned more easily, and could be produced at a fraction of the price of silver.

While Chase's actual name is the "Chase Brass and Copper Company," the products of this Waterbury, Connecticut firm are almost always referred to as "Chase Chrome" in the collecting field. Chase Chrome is by far the most popular of chromium housewares, and was produced from 1930 until 1941, when World War II forced the company to retool as a manufacturing plant for war materials. After the war, its housewares line was not revived.

The collecting field got its first boost in the late 1970s with a reprint of the full Chase catalogue for 1936–1937. It is easy to understand by this catalogue why Chase housewares were so popular. There was a wide variety of inexpensive, good-looking "Buffet Service Articles," " Decorative Items," "Drinking Accessories," "Lamps," "Smoker's Articles," and more. Chase had targeted the average American who was spending much more time entertaining at home during the Depression. Buffet-style parties suited America's informal lifestyle. Even Emily Post was enthusiastic about buffet gatherings, and heartily endorsed Chase's products.

However, it wasn't only the product line that made Chase so popular—it was the marketing of the line. Notable artists and industrial designers, including Lurelle

Guild, Rockwell Kent, Russel Wright, and Walter von Nessen were commissioned by Chase. The illusion of high style was completed by giving the products sophisticated names such as the "Diplomat" coffee set and the "Stratosphere" smoker stand. The image of the product was then underscored by the "Chase Shops," complete boutiques of Chase housewares, which were installed in major department stores in several parts of the country.

The collecting market for Chase is now firmly established. A series of books on collecting Chase have appeared over the years, including books by Richard Killbride, who was the first to identify many of the designers behind the Chase products, and several recent, excellent books co-authored by Donald-Brian Johnson and Leslie Pina.

People could not afford silver for their dining rooms and homes. Chrome, brass and copper were solutions for filling the gap. By the mid-1930s, almost any houseware item you can think of was available in chrome with colorful, ivory or black plastic handles: cocktail shakers, ashtrays, serving utensils, breakfast sets, trays, ice tongs, lamps, and cigarette boxes all sold widely. Most of these items originally sold for less than $1 to about $3, but some sold for the then high price of $7.50. Today, they can bring $30, $50, $200, $500, $1,000, or more.

The value of a piece of Chase Chrome depends on the designer, the strength of its design, its rarity, and its condition. When Chase was still plentiful on the market, much of it was showing up in mint condition in the original box—wedding presents that had been packed away generations ago. There are numerous resources available if you want to collect Chase Chrome: books, clubs, and Web sites. Pricing can vary greatly on Chase, and there are still bargains to be found, so it is still fun to hunt for it at shows and flea markets and on auction sites like eBay.

Rockwell Kent was one of the best-known artists of the 1930s. Kent designed only three items for Chase: a cigarette box, a wine cooler, and a wine bottle stand, all with a young Bacchus motif, and all are considered rare today. When these designs surged into the spotlight again in the late 1980s, the cigarette box and the wine cooler each

The Chase "Diplomat" tea service by Von Nessen has become an Art Deco icon. Courtesy of *decodame.com*, FL.

brought $2,000 at auctions. These prices seem to have come down a bit, although they are still among the highest-priced pieces of Chase other than cocktail shakers and sets.

Von Nessen's best contributions to the Chase line are also highly sought after today, and include the "Diplomat" tea service. This is one of the "chestnuts" of the chrome collecting field, of which there are now several. With its elongated, fluted styling and side pouring handles, it was one of the most popular Chase items, and was in production from the 1920s through the mid-1930s. He also designed the "Lazy Boy" and "Stratosphere" smoker stands, service dishes, cheese knives, cake trowels, trays, and more.

Chase's success created its own competition, and several other companies entered the market around the same time. Revere Copper and Brass Company entered the chrome housewares market in 1935 with seventeen designs by Norman Bel Geddes. Bel Geddes's design talents had already been recognized in furniture, graphics, and more. He was a household name after he designed the General Motors "Futurama" exhibit at the

1939 World's Fair. When Prohibition was repealed in 1933, the bar alternated with the buffet as the center of adult entertaining in the home. Many of Bel Geddes's chrome designs were bar accessories: trays, ice buckets, cocktail shakers, and more.

Revere also used evocative names, such as the "Manhattan" tray and cups with their "Skyscraper" cocktail shaker, and other pieces called "Penthouse," "Empire," "Aristocrat" and "Tuxedo." Revere also introduced its money-making line of copper-bottom saucepans with streamlined black handles, which are still favorites in the kitchen today.

Farber Brothers, a New York City company, used the trade name "Krome-Kraft" and sometimes "Silvercraft." A third brother, S.W. Farber, had his own company, and sold his chrome products under the trade name "Farberware." The Farber Brothers used many glass companies like the Cambridge Glass Company, Fostoria, Fenton, and even Corning-Pyrex to create the colorful ruby red, cobalt blue, and other colored glass inserts for their chrome holders, rims, and bases.

Many of the designs that were produced under the trade name "Krome-Kraft" are more traditional in nature, but there are a few Art Deco designs that collectors seek.

Manning-Bowman was another chrome manufacturer, today best known for its highly prized chrome mantel clocks, tea sets, and other housewares. Manning-Bowman had some outstanding modern designs in which tea set handles appear as black, angular wings on the pieces. In the late 1920s, they produced a type of chromium plate that was trademarked as Aranium. Their catalogue for 1934 celebrated the end of Prohibition with a cocktail service called "The Repealer." Their "Craftware" was a line of fluid, streamlined pieces.

Aluminum also came into use for housewares but, unlike chrome, it did not have the appearance of silver. Much of the popularity of chrome was based on the illusion of elegance that it maintained. Aluminum was lightweight, durable, and inexpensive, but it wasn't very "chic," and was only really used in industry until the late 1920s. However, toward the end of the 1930s and into the 1940s, when almost all metal was going to the war effort, chromium-plated housewares finally gave way to aluminum. Two of the biggest makers of aluminum home products toward the end of the Deco era were Kensington and West Bend, which often used the popular Art Deco motif of a penguin to decorate its products.

Interest in the aluminum collecting field has established itself over the past ten years, particularly in the pioneering aluminum designs of Russel Wright. Aluminum was also used by leading Modernist furniture designers such as Donald Deskey and Warren McArthur Corporation. However, good Art Deco housewares are more rare in aluminum, and much of the hammered aluminum that has become popular recently is more traditional, and some of it downright "homey" in design, far from the feeling of Art Deco urban sophistication.

When collecting chrome, try to buy only pieces in excellent to mint condition. The original box will have an added value to a collector. Make sure that the piece you are buying has its chrome plating intact. Chrome can be replated, but it is difficult and expensive, and dents are almost impossible to repair. Look also for cracks and chips to the plastic trim and handles, and inspect glass liners closely. Caring for chrome is easy—in fact, that was one of its strongest selling points in its heyday. Just some mild soap and water and a soft drying cloth will make it it look like you've been polishing silver all day.

The Cocktail Shaker Craze

Even if he isn't completely responsible for the fad of drinking martinis, one would have to say that collector Stephen Visakay is almost single-handedly responsible for the cocktail shaker collecting craze over the past ten years.

Since his first publication of a chapter in a book on Art Deco collecting about a decade ago, to his own book on the subject that appeared in 1997 and has been reprinted twice, to a nationwide touring museum exhibition featuring his collection along with reams of national publicity, Visakay managed to focus an entire market on the best of the best in Art Deco design for cocktail shakers and sets.

German airplane-shaped "traveling bars," ca. 1928, in silver-plated brass. Courtesy of Phillips, de Pury & Luxembourg, NY.

In the 1920s, martinis on the Upper East Side were being mixed in sterling silver cocktail shakers, while less wealthy folk were using glass or nickel-plated varieties. With the repeal of Prohibition in 1933, cocktail shakers started being manufactured by the thousands. While some companies continued making sterling or silver plate shakers, chrome-plated brass shakers were fast becoming the most popular.

Shapes and design motifs included skyscrapers and streamlined Art Deco forms, and others were shaped as penguins, bowling pins, roosters, barbells, and more. However, with the advent of World War II, the surging popularity of cocktail shakers came to a slow halt.

Notable designs were created by manufacturers such as International Silver Company, Chase, Revere, Farber Brothers, Manning Bowman and Napier, with much of the production centered in and around Meriden, Connecticut. Outstanding designers include Norman Bel Geddes, Lurelle Guild, Walter von Nessen, W. Archibald Welden, and Russel Wright. With few other references in the annals of American design, Emile A. Schuelke is at least noted as the designer of the now famous 1936 Napier "Penguin" cocktail shaker, which can sell today for $2,500 or more. Cocktail shakers and sets by these designers have become Art Deco icons because they represent outstanding design as well as an entire era of our social history.

The market shot skyward in June, 2001, when Visakay sold some of the best and rarest pieces from his collection at auction at Phillips, de Pury & Luxembourg in New York. The highest price was an almost unimaginable $44,000 for a 1920s German chromium cocktail set in the form of an airplane with a 17 1/2" wingspan. The plane disassembles into 23 components including spoons, cups, measures, and a shaker, and the wings themselves are flasks.

Other staggering prices achieved at that some auction include $16,000 for a similar German airplane set with a 12" wingspan; $22,000 for a 1930s Lurelle Guild cocktail set from International Silver in silver plate; and $13,000 for a 1936 Norman Bel Geddes "Manhattan" set with six cups from Revere in chromium-plated brass.

While the heat of the auction arena had something to do with these explosive prices, the best designs have not

Norman Bel Geddes, "Manhattan" cocktail set, ca. 1936 for Revere, in chromium-plated brass. Courtesy of Phillips, de Pury & Luxembourg, NY.

cooled off much since then. That's not to say that all Art Deco cocktail shakers are now floating in the stratosphere like one of the most sought-after designs, a Graf Zeppelin. Many good and better examples of Art Deco chrome, aluminum, and glass cocktail shakers and sets can still be purchased for under $300 to $1,000. It's also important to remember that no matter how expensive the cocktail shaker, the quality of the cocktails still depends on the bartender. ◙

9

GLASS

The growing recognition of the decorative arts, coupled with the emergence of the individual decorative artist in the mid-1800s, would be strongly reflected in the field of glass design. In addition, with the rise of urban areas, both art glass and functional glass were in high demand in the Art Nouveau and Art Deco periods.

As in the Art Nouveau period, the major center of glass production in France continued to be near the city of Nancy, in the Alsace-Lorraine region along the French border with Germany, with its rich forests to fire the furnaces. Czechoslovakia, where labor was cheap and raw materials abundant, became the other major center of European glass production, and much of the collectible Art Deco glass on the American market today is Czech.

In the United States, Art Nouveau glass is best known by the works of Tiffany and Steuben. Tiffany brought the United States unrivaled preeminence in stained and iridescent glass, and Tiffany lamps gain astronomical prices on the market today.

In the 1920s and 1930s, both in Europe and in the United States, mass-produced glass was needed to meet the demand of middle-class households. Handmade or studio production increasingly became economically unfeasible, and was carried on by only a few designers.

Glass is usually made from powdered flint or fine sand, ashes or another alkali, salt or metallic oxide, and lime. The type and proportion of its ingredients give it its color, transparency, opacity, ability to distort light, and so on. Lead crystal has at least 24 percent lead oxide. Other metallic oxides are what give color to glass.

The field of glass collecting in the Art Deco period is particularly rich and wide-ranging. One can collect many different kinds of glass: hand-blown, *pâte-de-verre*, cameo, enameled, acid-etched, leaded crystal, or molded—from a variety of designers and manufacturers. While prices for some artists and makers can be very high, many glass collecting areas are still accessible to beginning collectors looking for good examples of Art Deco.

Hand-Blown Glass and *Pâte de Verre*

The leading studio artists in hand-blown glass of the Art Deco period are Maurice Marinot, Henri Navarre, Andre Thuret, and Jean Luce. Blown glass is given its shape while still molten. Afterwards, surface decoration may be applied, painted, carved, or acid-etched.

Marinot's work, often deeply etched, was bought up by collectors and museums from the start. One of his hallmarks is the way he captured the air bubble in the glass. His style of glassmaking, where the artist and perhaps one or two assistants created the works, would soon give way to an increasingly industrialized glass manufacture using molds and power presses. However, it is interesting to note that the success of some of Marinot's design creations—especially the deep, acid-etched geometric patterns—would inspire others to create more Modernist designs to meet changing tastes and increasing demand. A selection of recent prices for works by Marinot at major auction houses have ranged from more than $7,000 for a 7" vase to more than $11,000 for an even smaller stoppered bottle.

In contrast to blown glass, *pâte-de-verre*, literally, "glass paste," is finely crushed glass crystals mixed with a binding agent. The paste is mixed with different metallic oxides for color, and can be sculpted in its cold state like clay and shaped into figures, plaques, bowls, or vases. The glass is then fired to re-vitrify the crystals. The result is a glass that can be decorated or colored throughout its mass, not just on the surface.

François Decorchement was the leading artist of the *pâte-de-verre* method. His work is rated on a par with the leading artists in other decorative arts of the period, and is rare and expensive on the market. Other notable *pâte-de-verre* artists are Gabriel Argy-Rousseau and Almeric Walter, who first ran the *pâte-de-verre* workshop at Daum and later set up his own company. Today, better examples of works by these artists are high priced on the collecting market.

A sampling of auction results for Decorchement over the past five years in American auction houses range from $1,400 for a small *pâte-de-verre* paperweight to close to $6,000 for a 6" vase. Works by Argy-Rousseau appear on the market more frequently and can command even higher prices. In the past three years, more than 100 works have appeared on the U.S. auction market, and have produced prices from $1,500 for a scarab pendant to just over $2,000 for a *pâte-de-verre* ashtray to more than $35,000 for a 9" vase, with many prices falling in the $5,000 to $10,000 range. Almeric Walter is known for his small figural *pâte-de-verre* dishes called *vide poche* in French, literally meaning "empty pocket," as these small dishes were used for spare change, keys, and other small items. Often molded with frogs, lizards, butterflies, and other creatures, these frequently sell in the $3,000 to $8,000 range at major auctions, but when a rare Walter *pâte-de-verre* and wrought iron handkerchief lamp came up at Sotheby's New York in June of 2003, it sold for $60,000.

Cameo Glass

Cameo glass was one of the first major types of glass to gain widespread popularity, and was revived in England in the 1870s. Cameo glass has two or more layers of superimposed glass, then the top layer or layers are carved to create the designs. At first carved by hand, glassmakers were soon using cutting wheels or etching the layers using hydrofluoric acid.

In the Art Nouveau period, Émile Gallé, one of the first glass artists to sign his work, created a style and technique for cameo glass that was widely copied. Both Gallé and another Alsatian glassmaker, Daum, were known for cameo glass using naturalistic motifs. As the Art Deco style emerged in France, a few glassmakers continued to create cameo glass, although it was far less adaptable to mass production than other methods.

The firms Degué and Legras made both cameo and acid-etched pieces, which are seen more frequently on the market, and are beginning to find a collecting base. The outstanding talent in cameo glass of the Art Deco period, however, is Charles Schneider, who trained under both Gallé and Daum, and founded Cristallerie Schneider in 1913.

His innovations in hand-crafted design and color would distinguish "Schneider" glass in its own right. Works thus signed generally tend to be uncarved pieces with a stylized simplicity of form and rich color, including deep greens, reds, blues, pinks, and an orange color he called "Tango."

Most sought after by Art Deco collectors today is a specialized cameo glass line Schneider called "Le Verre Français," literally, "The French Glass." The line included vases, lamps, bowls, urns, and more, usually acid-etched in highly stylized natural patterns of flowers and plants. Rarer, and more expensive, are the company's striking geometric patterns. Bright colors, such as red and orange, are highly prized, and some pieces also have applied handles and bases, often in a contrasting color.

Usually signed "Le Verre Français" in cameo, this line was also sometimes signed "Charder," an abbreviation of CHAR-les schnei-DER." Occasionally a piece will also

be signed "Ovington," the New York department store that helped popularize the line in this country, and for which Schneider created special commissions.

While the company continued to produce some art glass until 1982, it really flourished in the 1930s until the start of World War II. The bright colors were discontinued in 1933, due to the Depression and the rising costs of the rare minerals, such as uranium, needed to produce them. This was the case in both ceramics and glass worldwide, especially as uranium, which is the mineral for the color red, was put to wartime use.

Though production of Le Verre Français was to some degree industrialized, the quantity produced was much smaller than the mass production of Lalique and other glassmakers. The market for Le Verre Français began to take hold in the early 1980s following a major German museum exhibition. Much of the credit for its popularity is due to dealers Corey Warn and Mark Feldman of Antiquers III in Brookline, Massachusetts, who have specialized in Le Verre Français for close to three decades.

Another specialist dealer, Alain Fournier of La Verrerie d'Art, offers a wide selection of glass and ceramics on his Web site. Better examples of Le Verre Français can still be acquired in the $2,000–$3,000 retail price

A selection of Schneider glass, with several cameo-carved examples of "Le Verre Francais." Courtesy of Skinner, Inc., Boston.

A Daum acid-
etched vase, ca.
1930. Courtesy
of Bonhams &
Butterfields, CA.

range, but monumental and rare pieces can now command $8,000 to $10,000 or more. While still beyond the range of many collectors, prices for good and better examples of Le Verre Français today will appear modest ten years from now, and there are still bargains to be found in this collecting arena.

Acid-Etched Glass

In addition to cutting cameo layers, acid etching itself became a way of creating designs in thick-walled vessels made of a single layer of glass. The leading firm in the production of acid-etched glass in a modernistic style was Daum Nancy, which successfully made the transition to Art Deco with the new designs. Influenced by studio artists such as Maurice Marinot, Daum's larger production of geometrically etched vases, center-pieces, lamps, and other decorative pieces, was soon being sold through department stores on both sides of the Atlantic.

The market for acid-etched Daum started to emerge in the early 1980s, and today is fairly well established. Yet, because Daum is collected primarily for its Art Nouveau cameo glass pieces, bargains can still be found when buying its Art Deco geometric acid-etched pieces at auction, with many good examples coming in under the hammer at $2,000 or less. However, exceptional and monumental works can command much higher prices, such as a 14" vase that sold at Christie's in June, 2003 for more than $10,000 and an equally impressive acid-etched Daum table lamp that came in at $11,950.

Crystal

From the Scandinavian countries would come the best of yet another kind of glass: clear leaded crystal with modernist designs. As in other decorative arts, Scandinavian modern design in glass would have an impact in the United States. The leading Scandinavian crystal manufacturers were Orrefors, Leerdam, and Kosta.

Many talented designers worked for Orrefors during the 1920s and 1930s, including Simon Gate, Edward Hald, Vicke Lindstrand, and Nils Landberg. In the late 'teens, Orrefors developed "Graal," a cased glass in which colored relief decorations, such as fish swimming through sea grass, are covered with clear, smooth crystal. In 1936 a technique called "Ariel" was introduced, in which reflected light gives the impression of silver inside the glass, and the thick layers where air is trapped offer dazzling color. Both styles were popular for decades, having been produced beyond the Art Deco period, and in many instances not truly Art Deco in style. However, the earlier production is of interest to some Art Deco collectors, and Graal vases in many cases can still be purchased for less than $500. Ariel pieces, produced well into the 1970s, can command much higher prices.

Orrefors and Swedish glass got a noticeable boost in the market with the publication of several important books in the late 1990s, including *Orrefors Glass* (1995) by noted Art Deco expert Alastair Duncan, and *The Brilliance of Swedish Glass, 1918–1939* (1996), which accompanied a museum exhibition.

French firms offered some competition to the Scandinavians, perhaps most notably Baccarat. Founded in France in 1764, it continues today. In the 1920s, Baccarat produced some fine Art Deco designs, notably for perfume flasks and tableware in both glass and crystal, especially designs by Georges Chevalier. The Belgian firm Val St. Lambert, founded in 1825 and still in existence, created some striking Art Deco geometric cut crystal ware which is sought after.

In the United States, Frederick Carder established the Steuben Glass Company, absorbed by the Corning Glass Works in 1918. Carder's incredibly beautiful Art Nouveau iridescent designs wound up gathering dust on the shelves, as they were strongly challenged by the Scandinavians, and he was forced to make a transition to a new style. Some of Steuben's designs before 1930 fall broadly into what might be called an Art Deco style, though restrained, such as its "jade glass" vases with "alabaster" handles, made around 1925.

However, the best modern designs from Steuben started in 1931–1932, when Walter Dorwin Teague designed a series of crystal stemware patterns such as "Riviera," "Spiral," "Blue Empire," "Winston" and "St. Tropez." Teague was the firm's design consultant for only about two years, and his work for Steuben is highly collectible. Teague also designed for Libbey Glass Company, the leading producer of higher-quality everyday glassware in the 1930s.

A geometric cut crystal Belgian vase by Val St. Lambert, ca. 1930. Author's collection. Photo by Robert Four.

In 1933, just before opening its first New York City store on Fifth Avenue, Steuben commissioned John Gates and Sidney Biehler Waugh to create engraved designs in crystal that could compete with the Scandinavians. Waugh created massive vases with bold facets. He also used stylized mythological motifs carved into crystal, such as his "Europa" bowl and "Gazelle" bowl in 1935. Among other things, Gates designed The World's Fair Cup for the 1939 New York World's Fair, which incorporated the design of the Trylon and Perisphere on top. This, along with other designs, some monumental in size, were exhibited at the Steuben pavilion at the fair.

Collectors seeking good examples of Art Deco crystal and cut glass today should look to Czech glass for a more affordable place to start collecting. Perfume and toiletry bottles, decorative accessories, and striking Cubist geometric decanter sets can still be purchased, often for a fraction of the cost of "name brand" designs. Anonymously produced, Czech Art Deco glass was shipped in large quantities to the United States to be sold through both department and dime stores. However, the best examples are getting harder and harder to find. To collect the best Czech glass of the period, look for more intricate cutting and for better enameling without surface scratches. Lorial and Bryan Francis of *decodame.com* in Naples, Florida, almost always has striking examples of Czech Art Deco glass on offer.

Molded Glass—Lalique

Molded glass was the most suited to industrial mass production, and the maker who would rise to the very top of the industry was René Lalique, both because of his tremendous design talents and because he was the first to really accept and develop industrial mass production of glass, which helped lower prices and open up new markets. Lalique was a master artist, but his real genius was in staying ahead of the times.

Lalique actually started as an Art Nouveau jeweler, and had his first exhibition in Paris in 1890. His use of *pâte-de-verre*, enamels, rock crystal, and precious metals was immediately recognized for its genius, and brought him clients such as Cartier and Sarah Bernhardt. Somewhere around 1900 he starting to seriously create studio works in glass. At first he molded his designs in a *cire perdu*, or "lost wax," method like that used in bronze casting, and retained naturalistic motifs of humans, animals, and foliage in an Art Nouveau style. As he moved from this handcrafted style to more industrial production, his designs also changed to reflect newer styles.

The turning point came in 1907, when he was commissioned by Coty perfumes to design a line of scent bottles.

A Czech crystal decanter set, acid etched, with black and amber lacquer, ca. 1930s. Courtesy of *decodame.com*, FL.

Roger Coty was an entrepreneur with a great idea. Until this time, customers would have to bring their own bottles to the stores to be filled with perfume. What if, Coty thought, the perfume was sold in its own special bottle? For one thing, it would mean that perfume could be sold everywhere instead of in just a few places.

For Lalique, it was the right idea at the right time. Already very interested in glass, he now truly committed himself to it by setting up a factory for glass production near Paris in 1909. Since that time the bottle itself has been almost as important as the perfume inside in terms of making a sale. In 1920, Lalique acquired the company's present glass works in Alsace, right in the center of glass production in France.

Perfume and toiletry bottles have become a collecting field in themselves, and were produced by many notable Art Deco glassmakers including Gallé, Daum, Marinot, and Baccarat. Perfume bottles were also made in Germany, Sweden, and Czechoslovakia. The market for commercial perfume bottles has grown rapidly in the past two decades. Collectors especially look for perfume bottles that are "F.S.L.B."—filled, sealed, labeled, and boxed.

Generally, the shapes of Lalique's vases are simple, but the glass may be tinted in a variety of different colors, frosted or enameled. Molded designs can be in low, medium, or high relief. Motifs ranged from gods to geometric patterns to insects and fish, but most of his designs were drawn from nature. Especially popular are his figures and figurines of draped or nude women.

He created an incredibly wide range of products: picture frames, inkwells, glass table services, clocks, lamps and chandeliers, car radiator mascots, and perfume and toiletry bottles, which expanded his market and his popularity. Continually increasing his production, his line became available in quantity in both American and European department and jewelry stores. Vases, sculptures and other decorative objects, were popular gifts for weddings, anniversaries, and holidays. By 1933 he had produced more than 1,500 different items.

After his death in 1945, the family's artistic tradition was carried on by his son Marc, who reopened the factory,

A selection of patinated and frosted molded glass by Rene Lalique. Courtesy of Skinner, Inc., Boston.

which had closed in 1939 because of the war. Marc revived many of his father's designs as well as creating his own. Marc also changed the production from glass to lead crystal. Crystal has a content of at least 24 percent lead oxide, giving it greater weight and sparkle. More mid-century Lalique crystal is coming on the market today and creating its own generation of collectors.

When Marc Lalique died in 1977, he left the direction of the factory to his daughter Marie-Claude, who also designed sculptures, vases, and other items for exclusive distribution. The newer Lalique is sold under the trade name "Cristal Lalique," and is engraved "Lalique France," while works by René Lalique signed "R. Lalique," or "René Lalique." The company inscription has changed several times, and helps date a piece. For example, after 1950, pieces were signed "Lalique France," leaving off the "R," since Rene had died. If you intend to collect Lalique, it is best to arm yourself with a very good reference that shows signatures and marks.

Unfortunately, due to the popularity and high prices of Lalique, there are numerous fakes on the market. Sometimes the signature is all wrong or a fake is obvious because of poor quality or feeling very "lightweight," but in some cases the differences are more subtle and hard to discern. Because of this, caution is advised, and buying from a reputable source is of paramount importance. Also, because there is a quantity of Lalique available on the market, condition is of great importance to value. Pass by pieces that are chipped, cracked, or which appear ground down or polished.

The collecting base for Lalique, already large, got another boost in 1989 and 1990 when a major retrospective exhibition "Lalique: A Century of Glass for a Modern World" was organized by the Fashion Institute of Technology in New York, and traveled to museums in Coral Gables and Baltimore. Curated by Lalique expert and dealer Nicholas Dawes, it was the first major museum retrospective on Lalique since 1933.

Collectors who are interested in Lalique glass should not be daunted by the $10,000-plus prices that the best Lalique vases, jewelry, clocks, chandeliers, and sculptures can easily bring at auction, or the even rarer unique pieces that can bring $100,000 to $500,000. There is such a large quantity and range on the market, that good examples of Art Deco Lalique can often be bought for a few hundred dollars to just under $1,000.

For example, at the third annual Lalique Auction under the direction of Nicholas Dawes at David Rago Auctions in October, 2002, some vintage powder boxes sold in the $300 to $500 range; 1920s and 1930s bowls and center-bowls with striking designs sold from $600 to $900, and prices for early cake trays and serving plates started as low as $450. An opalescent Lalique bowl on a stand where it catches the sun can be a stunning addition to your Art Deco collection.

Molded Glass—Other Manufacturers

Though collected and collectible in their own right, with some commanding very high prices, a host of other makers of molded glass in both Europe and the United States will perhaps always be considered "imitators" of Lalique. These include French designers and firms such as Sabino, Etling, Hunebelle, Edouard Cazaux, Paul D'Avesn, and Muller Frères. Verlys, a French firm, transferred operations to the U.S. in the late 1930s until about 1951. The best-known American companies for this type of glass were Consolidated Lamp and Glass and Phoenix Glass, both of which produced "Lalique-like" molded and frosted glass.

Etling was an important manufacturer for the department store trade in the 1920s and 1930s, and was noted for its production of bronze and ivory statues and decorative ceramics as well as glass. André Hunebelle was a leading designer of tableware, and his designs tend to be more geometricized and abstract than Lalique's. After World War II, Hunebelle left the world of design and became a noted French film director. Striking Art Deco vases by Hunebelle can often be purchased for under $1,000.

Marius Ernst Sabino was a talented designer who exhibited at the 1925 Paris Exposition. He became known for his opalescent glass, which can be confusing for collectors as it continues to be produced today in a very Art Deco style. Except for some subtle color differences, many of the same models are still being produced. Muller Frères, while perhaps best known for their chandeliers and other lighting fixtures, also produced some striking vases, especially those incorporating metallic foil in the designs.

In the United States, Consolidated Lamp and Glass Company and Phoenix Glass, both located in Pennsylvania, also imitated Lalique for their molded vases.

Under the direction of chief designer Reuben Haley, Consolidated introduced its "Martelé," or hand-wrought, line of molded glass vases in 1926. The models reflected the influence of Lalique, and some, such as "Love Birds," were direct copies of the Lalique designs that Haley admired. When Consolidated closed from 1933 to 1936 because of the Depression, as many as forty to forty-five Consolidated molds were transferred to Phoenix, which continued their production under the direction of Reuben's son Kenneth Haley.

While the Consolidated and Phoenix molded vases were less well-executed both in color and quality than Lalique, they have created a fairly large collecting base that has expanded over the past decade. These Depression-era wares gained a popular market through the five-and-ten-cent stores at the same time Lalique's works were selling at fine department stores.

The collecting field for both Consolidated and Phoenix got a major boost in 1989 with the publication of Jack Wilson's book, *Phoenix and Consolidated Art Glass 1926–1980*, which still serves as the standard reference and describes in detail the company histories and offers profuse illustrations of the many lines and patterns they produced. Many Consolidated and Phoenix Lalique-style vases can still be bought for less than $500.

The most innovative, and truly American, design created by Reuben Haley for Consolidated, was the "Ruba Rombic" tableware line, introduced in 1928 and advertised as "An Epic in Modern Art." With its irregular Cubist-inspired geometric planes and angles, Ruba Rombic reflected the influence of jazz music on American design. Created in colors such as Jungle Green, Smoky Topaz, sunshine yellow, lavender, silver, and the rare, clear opal and black, it has become the most highly prized of all Consolidated designs.

There were about thirty-seven items in the Ruba Rombic line, and today many are so rare that only a few examples are known to exist, such as the 16 1/2" vase, and a fishbowl and stand that was actually produced by Phoenix, apparently under Kenneth Haley's direction. An example of the fishbowl and stand sold at auction in 2001 for $2,600. However, all Ruba Rombic must today be considered rare. The line was never produced again after Consolidated shut down in 1932 for a three-year duration.

In 1928 Kopp Glass, also of Pennsylvania, introduced its "Modernistic" vases, which resemble Ruba Rombic but have angular designs that are more regular. Reuben Haley also used the Ruba Rombic design for pottery produced by the Muncie Pottery Company of Muncie, Indiana, which is also difficult to find on the market today.

The first major exhibition and sale of Ruba Rombic, featuring more than 400 pieces, took place in September, 1992, at Moderne, a dealership in Philadelphia headed by Robert Aibel. Ruba Rombic pieces hardly ever come

up at auction. A three-piece dresser set with a toilet bottle, perfume, and tray all in lavender came up at Skinner in Boston in 1998 to sell for $5,750, and more recently one little whiskey glass sold for more than $100, also at Skinner. The small quantity of pieces that exist coupled with a high demand means that the best pieces will continue to appreciate in value. Estimates are that there are as few as 1,500 to perhaps as many as 3,000 pieces in existence. However, because the quantity available is so small, Ruba Rombic will never develop the wide collecting base that continues to fuel a very active market for Lalique, Daum, and other manufacturers.

A rare Ruba Rombic decanter set, 1928. Courtesy of Moderne, PA.

Depression Glass

In the 1920s and 1930s, "Carnival" and "Depression" glass flourished in America. Carnival glass, so-called because of its use as prizes at carnival booths, comes in a wide variety of shapes, patterns, and manufacturers. Carnival glass is not Art Deco in design. Rather, Carnival, with its metallic surface finish and iridescent color, is the Tiffany of carnival-goers.

Depression glass is the name given to a whole range of glass tableware produced to sell inexpensively during the Depression. Usually in transparent clear, green, pink,

amber, blue, and sometimes other colors, it was produced by numerous companies. Whole sets of this everyday kitchenware were given away as premiums with the purchase of a refrigerator or stove. Among the many companies that produced it are Indiana Glass Company, Anchor Hocking, Westmoreland, Hazel Atlas, and Federal.

While most Depression glass is not in the Art Deco style, there are a few patterns that Art Deco collectors widely seek, notably Indiana Glass Company's "Cracked Ice" pattern, "Pyramid" pattern, produced from 1928 to 1932, and its "Tea Room" pattern, produced from 1926 to 1931; Anchor Hocking's "Manhattan," produced from 1938–1939 to about 1943; and a design called "Cubist," produced by Jeannette Glass from 1929 to 1933.

Over the past decade, numerous collecting guides on Depression glass have been published, some helping to identify still more Art Deco patterns that have been overlooked from designers and manufacturers such as George Sakier for Fostoria Glass and Wilbur L. Orme for Cambridge Glass Company. Examples of Sakier's Art Deco designs for Fostoria Glass can be purchased for less than $100 and, in many cases, for less than $50. Much credit is due to author Leslie Pina, who has researched and published numerous collector guides that are invaluable for those seeking to collect Depression glass.

Depression glass is a collecting field unto itself, with thousands of collectors, clubs, and newsletters. Once you have decided on a pattern of Depression glass you'd like to collect, probably the best resources for building your collection are focused glass shows, big outdoor antique and collectible fairs such as Brimfield, or an auction Web site such as eBay, where thousands of Depression glass listings are posted every day. Also look around to see if there is a club or a Web site devoted to your choice—conventions, swap meets, and "want lists" can help build your collection and increase your enjoyment.

In general, the few Deco styles seem to bring higher prices than most general lines of Depression glass. While many examples of Art Deco Depression glass are still affordable at $25 or less, some prices have skyrocketed. For example, the rare and sought-after Pyramid ice bucket in yellow that sold ten years ago for $200–$250, now brings $750 or more, and a single 8 oz. Pyramid tumbler can command $150 or more. ◼

10

CERAMICS

Ceramics underwent the same transition as the other decorative arts, from artists creating new forms and decorations in the studio, to small-scale commercial production for the department store trade, and finally to inexpensive mass production. The Art Deco style brought a breakthrough in form, color, and subject. The ceramic artist was no longer limited to traditional vessels, jugs, bowls and tea sets, they could experiment with incised or painted decoration, modernist shapes, angularity, and subject matter, as sculptors were doing.

The diversity of the ceramics field in Art Deco makes it one of the most popular areas for collecting: from high-quality china and porcelain to earthenware pottery, from cloisonné enameled vases to industrially produced water jugs, fired and glazed in one step. And, while prices on some ceramics can be very high, it remains an area that is still accessible to beginning collectors looking for better examples of the Art Deco style.

A great starting place is Karen McCready's 1995 book *Art Deco and Modernist Ceramics*. When McCready died tragically in 2000 at age 54, her own collection, composed entirely of white ceramics, was donated to the Newark Museum, expanding even further its impressive Modernist holdings under curator Ulysses Dietz, who has headed the Decorative Arts Department since 1980.

French and Belgian Ceramics

Early Art Deco ceramic artists and studio potters in France included Émile Decoeur, Émile Lenoble, Henri Simmen, and René Buthaud. Buthaud's painted figures of women are reminiscent of Jean Dupas, and he was greatly influenced by African design motifs. These artists are rare on the open market today, and can command very high prices. Buthaud's vases easily sell on the retail market for $5,000 to $10,000, or even more.

Both Theodore Haviland's company and the French national manufacture, Sèvres, commissioned leading artists to decorate tablewares, usually of porcelain. Among the more famous are Jean Dupas, Jean Dufy, Robert Bonfils, Jacques-Émile Ruhlmann, and Suzanne Lalique, daughter of René Lalique.

Other fine studio artists whose work is sought after by collectors today include Jean Luce, Robert Lallemant, Raoul Lachenal, and André Méthey. Lallemant created innovative angular pottery, often with sporting motifs. Jean Mayodon's works for Sèvres, with their mythological and heroic figures, can sell for more than $20,000 at auction.

French department stores played an important role in popularizing ceramics production, as they had with other decorative arts. Maurice Dufrène of La Maitrise at the Galleries Lafayette, and Claude Lévy at the Primavera workshop of Printemps, both created and commissioned designs. Dufrène favored the ceramics of the Belgian company Boch Frères. Primavera carried so much Longwy that many pieces you'll find on the market today are marked "Primavera Longwy." Other leading design-

Cloisonné vases by Boch Freres and a trivet by Longwy, all circa 1930. Author's collection. Photo by Robert Four.

ers such as Jacques Adnet, known also for his furniture designs, also created ceramics for the department stores.

Figural ceramic sculptures distributed by the Parisian firm of Goldscheider and Fau & Guillard include Edouard Cazaux, André Fau, Lemanceau, and others. Some of these works are better examples of the Art Deco style and can be still found at affordable prices today.

Etling, too, seized upon the popularity of ceramics to produce figural ceramics by artists such as Joseph Descompes, and some work in the style of Longwy. Etling produced a great volume of decorative and functional glass, bronzes, and statues for the department stores.

Both the Belgian firm Boch Frères and the French manufacturer Longwy produced decorative ceramics using the cloisonné enamel technique, which had come into commercial production as early as 1870. Their highly stylized natural and geometric designs in striking colors, usually on a crackled white or ivory ground, were achieved by using enamel glazes separated from one another by a material that resists their running together when fired.

Until the Art Deco period, Longwy's work was largely influenced by Far and Near East patterns. Longwy is the only firm in France still producing ceramics in cloisonné enamel. Richard Fishman, owner of As Time Goes By in

San Francisco, has made a decades-long specialization in Boch Frères and Longwy, and even commissioned the company to create ceramic tiles for his storefront and special-edition pieces for his store in cloisonné enamel.

Charles Catteau was the chief designer for the Belgian firm Boch Frères during the Art Deco era. Those works stamped with Charles Catteau's signature, especially when decorated with sleek deer and other animals, are the most sought after in today's market. New books and documentation on Boch Frères , sponsored by the Belgian government, have brought to light the wide and important range of its production. In addition, plans are underway to open a new museum of Boch Frères in Belgium in 2006, accompanied by the most comprehensive book to date. These developments will surely impact the collecting market for Boch Frères .

The collecting base is still relatively small, and better examples are still within reach, although the best pieces have started to climb quite high. Good examples of Boch Frères vases bring $350 to $750, better examples $750 to $1,500, and many rare pieces, especially those with figural designs, are now bringing $2,000 and more. Truly unique and rare pieces can bring far above that amount.

In Paris, another retailer, Robj, is best known on the market for its humorous decanters representing people from all walks of life. Robj also produced *bibelots*, or "knick-knacks": statuettes, lamps, bookends, ashtrays, and candy dishes. Even the tradition-loving Quimper pottery produced a line called "Odetta" in an Art Deco style to compete with the times.

German, Austrian and Czech Ceramics

The Germany company Rosenthal produced porcelain figures, vases, covered boxes, and other decorative items for the department store trade, often painted with stylized natural and geometric patterns. Their figures are often modeled as Pierrots, women in modern dress, and animals. Rosenthal pieces are almost always identified by the factory stamp.

German tablewares in the late 1920s and early 1930s were inspired by the functional aesthetic of the Bauhaus, sometimes with abstract geometric decorations. One of the major manufacturers of tableware in this style was Villeroy & Boch. Be careful, however, of recent Villeroy & Boch designs that simply echo the Art Deco style.

In Austria, the firm of Goldscheider (which also had a branch in Paris) was well known for bronze and bronze and ivory statues, and also created porcelain and ceramic decorative figures. Often the same artists, such as Lorenzl, were commissioned to create models for both bronze and ceramic production. Figures include dancers, nude maidens, sleek animals, and women in modern dress. Often seen in the market are Goldscheider's wall-mounted sculptures of women's heads, which have recently brought $600 to $1,000 at auction.

Another firm, Augarten, also produced figural porcelains in the Art Deco style starting in about 1922, and commissioned artists such as Wiener Werkstätte ceramist Valerie (Vally) Wieselthier to produce models.

Barely visible on the Art Deco collecting scene a decade ago, Czech ceramics, often with striking Cubist shapes and geometric painted surfaces, are widely found today. Like their Czech glass counterparts, most of these wares were produced anonymously and in fairly large quantities for export to the American dime store market. Colorful and affordable, they are popular with beginning and advanced collectors alike. Better examples of Czech ceramics can still be purchased for less than $500.

Swedish Ceramics

Gustavsberg pottery began producing modernist ceramics in 1917 under the artistic direction of Wilhelm Kage. In tablewares, Kage introduced his decorative "Worker's Service" in 1917, and his functional "Praktika Service" in 1933, influenced by the Bauhaus. Most Scandinavian pottery of the period does not fit the definition of "Art Deco," but perhaps best known to Art Deco collectors is Kage's "Argenta" stoneware. Introduced in the late 1920s and in production until the 1950s, it usually has a green mottled glaze with designs in overlaid silver of fish, mermaids, and other motifs. "Argenta" appears fairly frequently on the Art Deco market, but still seems to attract few collectors, with many of the prices thus remaining within reach. Good examples of the style can

still be purchased for well under $500, and better examples can be acquired for less than $1,000.

British Ceramics

In the world of Art Deco British ceramics, Clarice Cliff leads the market, along with a more recent but tremendous upsurge of interest in the ceramics of Susie Cooper. Cliff signed on with A. J. Wilkinson, and from 1916 to 1920 began experimenting in decorating old stock at the nearby Newport Pottery Company, which was later bought by Wilkinson.

In all, she created, or directed the creation of, about 250 shapes and more than 200 different paint designs for vases, jugs, tableware, coffee sets, and more. She commissioned other artists such as Laura Knight, Vanessa Bell, Graham Sutherland, Milner Grey, and Eva Crofts.

Her pottery was first exhibited in this country at the groundbreaking Minneapolis Institute Art Deco revival exhibition in 1971. It occupied a good portion of the ceramics section, but did little to awaken interest in the collecting arena. She created bold designs with brilliant colors in motifs often borrowed from Cubism as well as

"Bizarre"
demitasse set by
Clarice Cliff, ca.
1930. Author file
photo.

from ancient Egypt. Her brightly painted fantastic scenes with blobby trees were also perhaps inspired by Matisse and the Fauves.

The market for Clarice Cliff in the United States was initially driven by dealers Susan and Louis Meisel. Their groundbreaking book on Cliff entitled *A Bizarre Affair: The Life and Work of Clarice Cliff*, published in 1988, caused a surge of interest. The Clarice Cliff collecting field has been expanding ever since, and numerous reference books now exist. The large volume of production available has created an enormous collecting base, with collector clubs, dedicated Web sites, and even a market for reproductions.

Early on, savvy dealers in Cliff bought up vast quantities of her work by running small classified ads in Australian newspapers, a continent to which much of her production had been exported. Today, better individual pieces of Cliff's pottery can bring very high prices, from $2,500 to $5,000 and more. Dealers such as Carole Berk in Maryland have had long-standing strong specialties in her work. While the market in the United States is firmly established, most auctions of her work still take place in England. Dedicated collectors might find it worth the trip to travel to the specialized Cliff auctions at Christie's South Kensington, in England.

In 1929 Cliff's "Bizarre" ware, designed for Wilkinson, was growing in popularity, and the company devoted the entire production of Newport Pottery Company to its manufacture. Bizarre has several painted patterns, such as "Tennis," "Delicia Citrus," "Lugano," "Autumn," and many others. Although collectors of Cliff today ask for it by pattern name, and even model numbers, generally you'll hear the entire line referred to as simply "Bizarre." Another Cliff line that has several pattern names is called "Fantasque."

The vivid colors which were the source of her popularity were also probably the tragic cause of her death. Bright red in both ceramics and cameo glass production is toxic, as it is created from uranium oxide, the use of which was largely halted when uranium came under the control of the military in World War II. Its use in designs such as her important Deco pattern "Sunray" probably hastened her death by emphysema.

Other British ceramic designers working in modern idioms were Keith Murray and Eric Slater. Keith Murray, an architect who also created glass designs for Stevens & Williams, was hired by Wedgwood in 1932. Wedgwood needed a competitive edge in the 1930s market, and Murray provided it with simple shapes and solid light-colored glazes, often with horizontal banding, as well as designs in deep brown and black basalt. Vases by Murray in this style can often be purchased for less than $500, but some rare and large works can be priced up to $2,000. Note that the more sought-after pieces produced before World War II are marked with Murray's complete signature stamp, whereas later production is marked with a circular stamp bearing only his initials.

Eric Slater took over the position of art director at Shelley in 1928, a position once held by his father. He produced some of the best modern designs for that company throughout the 1930s, including porcelain tea sets with geometric decorations and angular handles. In 1937–1938 he was also commissioned to produce tablewares for Imperial Airways. Shelley's Art Deco tea and coffee sets are quite attractive and can be inexpensive, but they hardly ever show up in the American market.

The Art Deco designs of Charlotte Rhead for Burgess & Leigh, Poole Pottery, and Wiltshaw & Robinson's "Carlton Ware" have been steadily gaining their share of the

British collecting market, but haven't yet made great inroads in the United States. Better examples of Poole Pottery can still be purchased for $250 to $500, and can have wonderful Art Deco painted decorations.

American Ceramics

Rookwood, Van Briggle, Greuby, and Newcomb were some of the ceramic producers represented at the 1900 Exposition Universelle in Paris, and won many prizes. These makers and others are vied for in the Arts and Crafts market. Of them, only Rookwood went on to create notable Art Deco designs by artists such as William Hentschel, Sara Sax, Elizabeth Barrett, and Harriet Wilcox. Hentschel's airbrushed and stenciled Art Deco designs are particularly prized. This production, which ended in 1932 when all of the decorators were laid off in the Depression, is increasingly sought after. These are difficult to find, but usually cost far less than comparable quality Arts and Crafts Rookwood, and can be quite stunning.

Fulper Pottery also sometimes exhibits the simplified lines of Art Deco, and later, around 1930, did produce some striking modern pieces. Overbeck Pottery was founded in Cambridge City, Indiana, in 1911 by four sisters, and created some outstanding Art Deco designs. However, production was small and, for the most part, these are never seen on the market.

While the academic foundations for a modern ceramics movement were strong in America, the arrival of World War I slowed down ceramic development. Between the two wars, especially in Cleveland, Ohio, American ceramics underwent dramatic changes. Students at the Cleveland Institute of Arts came under the influence of a Viennese teacher, Julius Mihalik, who exposed them to the thinking of the Wiener Werkstätte.

Outstanding students from the school included Thelma Frazier Winter, Paul Bogatay, and Edris Eckhardt, all of whom would later design for Cowan Pottery Company, located in a suburb of Cleveland. Many other young ceramists from the Midwest, including Russel Aitken and Viktor Schreckengost, traveled to study in Vienna.

These Cleveland artists started a renaissance in American ceramics. Even though many won prizes, and annual

exhibitions were held starting in 1919, their work was largely ignored. In 1926, the Metropolitan Museum of Art's show largely consisted of French ceramics. In 1928, when the Metropolitan hosted the International Exhibition of Ceramic Art, the work of the Wiener Werkstätte and many Americans finally came to the fore.

The artists recognized in this exhibit are also the most popular on today's market: Henry Varnum Poor, William Zorach, Carl Walters, William Hunt Diederich, and Viktor Schreckengost. Another important ceramic artist was Maija Grotell, who was associated with the Cranbrook Academy of Art.

Susi Singer and Vally Wieselthier, notable Austrian Wiener Werkstätte ceramists, emigrated in 1932. Singer settled on the West Coast, and Wieselthier received commissions from Contempora and General Ceramics in New York, and Sebring Pottery in Ohio.

It is interesting to note that neither of the two most important Art Deco revival exhibitions in this country, "Art Deco" at the Finch College Museum, and "The World of Art Deco" at the Minneapolis Institute of Arts in 1971, included American potters and ceramists. In Minneapolis, German, British, and even Japanese stood side-by-side with the French, but the only identifiably American company represented, and only with a single piece, was the American Art Clay Company.

Examples of Roseville "Futura", 1928, Keith Murray for Wedgwood, and Poole Pottery. Author's collection. Photo by Robert Four.

Many of the American artists mentioned above were to become part of what would be America's most successful Art Deco ceramic enterprise: Cowan Pottery Studios in Ohio. Founded in 1921 by Reginald Guy Cowan, a successful studio ceramist whose work had won awards as early as 1917, it drew together talented young artists such as Russel B. Aitken, Arthur E. Baggs, Alexander Blazys, Waylande DeSantis Gregory, Paul Manship, A. Drexler Jacobson, Margaret Postgate, and Viktor Schreckengost.

Cowan produced both limited editions and larger series of decorative and functional ceramics that have become highly prized in the Art Deco collecting world. The firm lasted about twelve years. At its largest, it had about 1,400 dealer outlets nationally including Marshall Field of Chicago, Wanamaker's of Philadelphia, and Halle's of Cleveland. Commercial production increased, but smaller editions of ceramic sculptures continued to be made. Then, financial difficulties caused the company's failure during the Depression. Interestingly, many great, stylish pieces were created in 1930 and 1931, when the company was in receivership and the artists were finally free from the pressures of commercial production.

R. Guy Cowan's most popular creation was the figural "flower frog." These are ceramic stylized women and animals rising from lily pads and grasses. Set in a shallow bowl of water, holes in the base make it possible to arrange flowers in the piece. He designed numerous other pieces for Cowan Pottery Studio, but most are not signed as his designs.

Almost as prolific as Cowan himself was Waylande Gregory, who joined the firm in 1928. When it closed, Gregory continued producing ceramics under his own name from his studio at the Cranbrook Academy of Art. Gregory often took subjects from mythology and history, such as "Persephone" and "Salome." He even depicted "Radio" as a woman in white ceramic, hair blowing at right angles in the wind, and the famous Deco zigzag bolt emanating from her fingertips. During Prohibition, the favorite Gregory designs were "King and Queen" decanters, inspired by "Alice Through the Looking Glass," and disguised as bookends.

Gregory also designed the "Fountain of Atoms," a monumental ceramic sculpture for the New York World's Fair, with twelve figures, each weighing more than a ton. The work was commissioned by the Works Progress Administration, or WPA, under its Welfare Arts Program. The Ceramics Division for this program was set up in Cleveland.

Viktor Schreckengost joined Cowan in 1930 and created numerous outstanding designs. Best known is his bowl called the "Jazz Bowl," now an icon of American Art Deco design. The Jazz Bowl is decorated with Jazz Age designs of New York on New Year's Eve: skyscrapers, neon signs, cocktail glasses, and street lamps. It was created using the *sgraffito*, or drypoint, technique, where the design is scratched on the surface by hand before firing, making each piece unique. Schreckengost perfected the technique, and Arthur Baggs perfected the glaze, known as "Egyptian Blue." Only about fifty of the bowls were made in this manner, and two were purchased by Eleanor Roosevelt, who had commissioned the design.

At the Cincinnati Art Galleries Keramics Auction 2000, a rare example of the Jazz Bowl sold for $121,000 to the Cleveland Museum of Art, which featured it in the retrospective exhibition, "Viktor Schreckengost and 20th-Century Design, which took place the same year. (See the Recognizing Art Deco chapter for a picture of the Jazz Bowl.)

In 1931 Schreckengost created a slightly smaller variation of the Jazz Bowl with a flared rim. For this production, which only resulted in about twenty bowls being made, the design was modeled in low relief so it did not have to be done by hand. An example of this Jazz Bowl sold at David Rago's 20th-Century Modern Auction in October, 2000, for $53,000, and another example brought $68,150 at Christie's in 2001. Ironically, Schreckengost had nicknamed this version "The Poor Man's Bowl," because it was so much less expensive to produce!

While the Jazz Bowl holds the record for an American Art Deco ceramic work at auction, many good and better examples of Cowan Pottery can still be purchased in the $200 to $1,000 range. Strong figural works are among the best examples and command the highest prices,

Cowan "King and Queen" decanters and flower frogs by Waylande Gregory and "Push Pull" elephant bookends by Margaret Postgate. Author's collection. Photo by Robert Four.

often as high as $2,000, with the rarest works even higher.

The most outstanding collection of Cowan in America is at the Cowan Museum at the Rocky River Public Library in a western suburb of Cleveland, Ohio. With an active support group, the Cowan Museum Associates, the museum hosts a symposium each year on Cowan Pottery, usually followed by an auction that benefits the collection. The collecting base for Cowan has expanded and prices have increased since the publication of the outstanding 1998 reference *Cowan Pottery and the Cleveland School*, by Mark Bassett and Victoria Naumann Peltz.

Roseville Pottery Company of Ohio annually produced lines of ceramics, often with flowered patterns. While many of its designs show some Art Deco influence, its "Futura" line, introduced in 1928, is the most distinctive and the most sought after on the Art Deco market. The line experimented with form as well as glaze, creating odd-angled and geometric vases with angular handles, stepped-back skyscraper forms on necks and bodies, and glaze combinations such as green and orange, and green and pink. Good examples of Futura can still be purchased for well under $500, better examples for less than $1,000, and some of the best for less than $2,000. However, one very rare piece sold for $9,500 at David Rago Auctions in 2001.

Other American ceramics firms that produced decorative work in the Art Deco style include the American Art Clay Company of Indianapolis, or AMACO, as its pieces are often signed. Not frequently found on the market, its best pieces can command several hundred dollars, and is notable for the quality of its glazes, which are often finely crazed.

Frankoma Pottery, which started in the mid-1930s in Oklahoma and is still in operation today, created some Modernist designs in their single-handled, lidless water pitchers. Decorative glazing techniques included a brushed glaze in green and copper colors, sometimes called "Prairie Green," and high-luster black glazes with metallic tones. It is difficult to date Frankoma, as its most popular glazes are still being used today.

In New Jersey, Lenox, which was founded under another name in 1889 in Trenton, produced interesting figural and functional Art Deco ceramics, as did Trenton Art Pottery, which operated in the 1930s and into the 1940s. Generally, Trenton pieces are geometric spheres and circles, unadorned, with pastel glazes in yellows, blues, greens, and pinks. As previously mentioned, General Ceramics of New York also produced decorative wares, notably those designed by Vally Wieselthier.

Though much of its production was after World War II, Red Wing Pottery has some nice Art Deco designs that are still very affordable. If you are going to collect Red Wing, arm yourself with one or more books by the indefatigable Red Wing advocate Ray Reiss.

Mass-produced ceramic tableware and kitchenware were the final outcome of the transition from early Art Deco to industrialized production. Robert T. Hall of Hall China in East Liverpool, Ohio, developed a single-step glaze which would withstand kiln-firing at high temperatures, and brought the price of functional ceramics down dramatically. Durable and practical, it was first sold to restaurants and hotels, and later retailed in department stores.

Among the most collectible Hall items are the late 1930s "Refrigerator Ware" leftover dishes and water pitchers designed for appliance manufacturers such as Westinghouse and Hotpoint. These were given away as premiums with the purchase of a new refrigerator, and are colorful and stylish. Also popular are streamlined and stylized teapots such as "Aladdin," "Surfside," "Airflow," and rare works with novelty forms such as "Automobile," "Basketball," "Doughnut," and "Football." Better Hall pieces, especially in hard-to-find colors can range in price upward of $500.

Hall withdrew from the retail market in the 1950s, due to low sales caused mostly by cheap Japanese ceramics, and returned to producing restaurant wares. However, in 1984 it reintroduced many of its Art Deco styles to the public, and even included a new line of plates and platters for microwave ovens. All of the molds for the 1,100-plus pieces Hall ever made were still in storage, and many are being reissued—in more than 100 colors—so buyer beware.

Homer Laughlin introduced Frederick H. Rhead's "Fiesta" dinnerware in 1936, and their "Harlequin" pattern in 1938. "Fiesta" was produced continuously from 1936 through 1972, and reintroduced again in 1986. Pre–World War II colors were red, blue, yellow, green, and ivory, with turquoise added in 1938. Red was discontinued in 1943 because of the war, due to the uranium oxide used to produce it, but was reintroduced in 1959. New colors are pastel shades of apricot, rose, and sea mist, plus a cobalt blue, black, and white. Again, it is up to the collector to know which colors are the original line.

Cheaper and cheaper ceramics with Deco styling were produced, including the swarms of pink flamingoes that flew home from Florida in tourists' baggage. Much of this production can still be found in flea markets and fairs, and some of it is interesting, decorative, and functional. Recently, there has been a huge surge of interest in, and collecting of, California pottery of the period, which can often have "echoes of Deco."

In 1937, Russel Wright was commissioned by Steubenville Pottery Company to create a line of tableware that he called "American Modern." In some ways this style still reflects the Streamline design of late 1930s, but it was really more a precursor of the Biomorphism of the 1940s, along with tableware designs by Eva Zeisel and chairs by Charles and Rae Eames. By the end of the 1930s, designers were already abandoning the Art Deco style, and Biomorphism would soon overtake it. In 1941, the Museum of Modern Art hosted the first exhibition of this new design style, which it called "Organic Design." As a final blow to Art Deco, Russel Wright's American Modern tableware was ultimately produced in plastic. ◙

11

PRINTS AND GRAPHICS

Lithographs, wood engravings, and etchings, especially those that are hand signed by the artist from a limited edition, are generally considered "fine art prints." However, Icart's hand-signed etchings are often sold at Art Deco "decorative art" auctions, and advertising posters of the 1920s and 1930s, which were also usually lithographs, will today often be described as "fine art posters," emphasizing the high quality of their design and printing method.

Again, in this collecting arena as in the world of Art Deco sculpture, there was a closer *rapprochement*, or coming together, of the fine arts and applied arts than ever before. Fine artists were commissioned to produce advertising posters. Textile designers and fashion magazine illustrators also sometimes issued signed, limited-edition decorative prints to be sold through galleries. Painters sometimes turned to printmaking as a means of more affordably disseminating their work, and during the WPA, they often took commissions to produce prints just to keep food on the table. In fact, about the only common ground all of these areas share is that they are "on paper."

Fine Prints

In Europe and America there were numerous notable fine print artists whose works are today collected in the Art Deco arena. In addition to Louis Icart, who is perhaps the best known to Art Deco collectors, French artists such as Raoul Dufy, Marie Laurencin and Jean-Émile Laboureur are sought after for their "look" as much as for their artistry and technique. Laboureur's figures are particularly "Deco" in their stylization and often in their costume, much like the works of his colleague Jean Dupas. Happily, good and better examples of signed prints by these and other period French artists can still be purchased for less than $2,000.

American fine print artists—especially those depicting urban, Machine Age subjects such as Howard Cook, Louis Lozowick, Otis Oldfield, and Harry Sternberg— can be very expensive to acquire. Over the past two decades, as American art museums have seriously begun collecting works by early 20th-century artists, the prices on these and many others have risen rapidly. Several prints by Cook, Lozowick, and others, especially those depicting New York scenes, can now command from $3,000 up to $10,000 and more.

Lithographs and wood engravings by another notable American artist, Rockwell Kent, have perhaps an even more direct visual appeal to those who appreciate Art Deco. His wood engravings are among the most expensive of his prints, now often selling in the $3,000 to $5,000 range. Kent's numerous illustrated books, such as *N. by E.* (1930), are also popular with Art Deco collectors. Books illustrated by British wood engraver Clare Leighton are also sought after, as are the stunning woodcut novels by American artist Lynd Ward, which convey

"La Peche,"
a woodcut by
Raoul Dufy,
1910. Author's
collection.
Photo by Robert
Four.

their entire book-length story through a series of images without using a single word of text. Many good and better first editions of books illustrated by these and other Art Deco period artists can still be acquired for less than $500.

Other American artists of the period worth looking for include Chicago artists Charles Turzak and William S. Schwartz; California wood engraver Paul Landacre; lithographer Jan Matulka; early works by Philadelphia artist Benton Spruance; and New York and urban scenes by Jolan Gross Bettelheim, James E. Allen, Martin Lewis, and several others. While these artists can bring high prices for their best work, by far the most expensive is Martin Lewis, whose etchings have soared in the past decade, with rare works now bringing $20,000 and more.

Other European printmakers to look for include British wood engravers: Eric Gill, whose works often have a Gothic feeling to them, and John Buckland Wright. Lithuanian Boris Lovet-Lorski, known primarily as a sculptor, also created two portfolios of lithographs that are sought after for their stylized figures of horses and nudes.

One common element to all of the artists cited above is that their work is primarily figurative, rather than abstract. While Cubism and other abstract art movements are certainly reflected in the fine prints of the day, it is this figurative stylization that has caused these artists to have "crossover" appeal to Art Deco collectors.

Louis Icart

Louis Icart arrived in Paris in 1907, but cutting-edge art movements such as Cubism had little influence on Icart's romantic style. Icart began as an apprentice fashion designer, and was drawn to the female form. Etchings of women would be his formula for commercial success.

He chose his women from legends, operas, and the day's entertainers and celebrities. Their elongated figures are exaggerated even further by their lounging positions. Icart's women are also often accompanied by greyhounds or other dogs, and their long furs and high heels show that they were women of some means. You won't find any harsh zigzags or bold geometric patterns in Icart etchings, just soft, stylish curves.

He first exhibited in the United States in 1922 at John Wanamaker's department store in New York. In 1925 printmaker Anton Schutz, who had a business called the New York Graphic Art Society, negotiated the exclusive distribution of Icart's work in America. Schutz created The Louis Icart Society, and soon Icart became the wealthiest artist in France.

At the height of his career, tens of thousands of etchings had been exported to the U.S. According to a 1933 catalogue, most of these sold for $12 to $15, with some as high as $20. They were popular during the Depression for their gaiety and color. However, when the war broke out, Icart could no longer obtain copper for etching plates. After the war, the world and the market had changed, and his etchings had lost their appeal. Though he made a promotional tour of America in 1948, his popularity was over as suddenly as it had begun. When he died in 1950, many of his works could be bought for pennies.

Since the revival of his popularity in the 1960s, prices for his work overall have risen dramatically, but his prices seem more susceptible than most to the rise and fall with the general Art Deco market. There was a surge of buying in the early 1990s, with some prices reaching more than $20,000 at auction. That upward trend truly crashed in the face of an economic recession, and the Japanese, who had been among the strongest buyers, suddenly lost their "yen."

His most popular etching called "Vitesse," or "Speed," was produced in two different versions. Created originally in 1929, it shows a woman with three greyhounds on leashes, and the gray greyhound leads the pack. Re-etched in 1933, the black dog is in the lead. Thousands of copies of "Vitesse" were sold, and they still command good prices on today's market, with examples bringing $2,000 to $3,500 at auction in recent years.

Today, however, the bloom is largely off the rose. There is a volume of his work on the market, and numerous good examples can be acquired at auction for under $1,000. Even better examples, such as "My Model," "The Sofa,"

"Spring Blossoms," and "Joie de Vivre" have sold at auction between $2,500 and $3,500 recently, less than half of what they once realized. However, the best still do sell at $5,000 and higher, such as a rare example of the 1935 "Follies Follies" showing a chorus girl kickline, which brought more than $9,000 at Sotheby's in 1995, and the 1934 "Leda and the Swan," which soared to $12,650 at the same auction house a year later. Icart's early French distributor, L'Estampe Moderne, listed forty-two works in their 1922 catalogue. These were printed in editions of 300 each and the copper plates were then scratched with an "X" to prevent further printing. To help authenticate them, look for a pencil signature and the blind stamp of a windmill embossed into the paper in the margin.

The actual quantity of impressions of later works is harder to establish. The Louis Icart Society reissued many of his most popular designs at the time to meet the demand. Also, some of his copper plates were steel- or nickel-plated to allow for additional printing. Many of his works were registered with the U.S. Copyright Office by numerous distributors: F.H. Bresler Company of Milwaukee, the Louis Icart Society, his French publishers L'Estampe Moderne and Gravures Modernes. The copyright can usually be found in the top right or left corner, however a number of the copyrights were renewed after his death and are still active.

Louis Icart, "Leda and the Swan," etching, 1934. Courtesy of Bonhams & Butterfields, CA.

The best single resource book is *Louis Icart: The Complete Etchings*, published in 1990 by Schiffer but still in print, which has given collectors and dealers a new reference tool for identifying more than 500 Icart etchings.

French Advertising Posters

Graphic design changed to attract wider markets to the host of new products being offered. In Europe, posters were an effective way of reaching mass audiences, but modern posters had to be strong enough to be read from passing cars, capturing attention with typography, the image, bold lines and colors, short messages, and interesting angles.

Early color lithography was a cumbersome process of drawing with grease pencil on heavy slabs of Bavarian limestone. One stone for each color was needed to achieve the desired effect. In the 1870s, Jules Chéret, called "The Father of the Pictorial Poster," greatly advanced color lithography. The finest posters of the Art Deco era were also color lithographs, usually rendered on zinc plates rather than on limestone. Commercial printing soon became a photographic plate process, and offset printing became popular. Some posters were "photo-montage" designs, incorporating both photographs and lithography with startling, eye-catching effects. Ultimately, the photographic image—of a product, a resort, or a performer—finally overcame the hand-illustrated image.

Early lithographic posters will generally always be more valuable than photo offset posters, no matter who the artist, although there can be exceptions. When in doubt about the printing technique used, look at the poster under a jeweler's lens or any strong magnifier. Photographic printing is really achieved by a series of straight lines and tiny color dots that can be discerned on close inspection.

Often elongated and condensed, the new typography lent itself to the new sense of speed that dominated graphic design. Many of the new typefaces were sans serif, that is, the letters did not have little feet. Popular new styles included Paul Renner's "Futura" (1928), Koch's "Kabel" (1927), Eric Gill's "Gill Sans" (1928), and others such as "Bifur," "Bauhaus," and "Broadway," a decidedly American Art Deco type style. In looking at Art Deco posters, notice how much the typography can impact the overall visual appeal. Other artistic and design movements, such as the Vienna Secession, Cubism, and Futurism would have a profound impact on advertising design.

The best-known and overall highest-priced French Art Deco posterist is A. M. Cassandre. Cassandre influenced an entire generation of graphic designers, both in France and abroad. Though he won the Grand Prix for poster design at the 1925 Paris Exhibition, and had a prolific career, it was not until 1951 that the Musée des Arts Decoratifs held a retrospective of his work. He also produced magazine covers and illustrations for *Harper's Bazaar*, *Fortune* and others. His fame today means these are snatched up quickly at strong prices.

Cassandre's poster for the "Normandie," 1935. Private collection. Photo by Robert Four.

By subject, travel posters are the most highly realized Art Deco designs, and Cassandre was the master of these. His posters include many for ocean liners and trains: "Étoile du Nord" (1927), "Nord Express" (1927), "L.M.S. Bestway" (1928), "L'Oiseau Bleu" (1929), "Chemin de Fer du Nord" (1931), "L'Atlantique" (1931), "Wagon Bar" (1932), and "Normandie" (1935). Almost all of these posters now sell for $10,000 or more, and some of his posters have sold in excess of $30,000 at auction.

Pierre Fix-Masseau, whose style is similar to Cassandre's, is also best known for his train posters. His well-known and often-reproduced "Exactitude" poster sold for $11,500 at auction in 2003 at Swann Galleries.

Other than Cassandre and Fix-Masseau, the best known Art Deco travel posterist is Roger Broders. Known for his highly stylized and colorful destination posters for the French Riviera and other destinations, many of his posters today sell in the $3,000 to $5,000 range, and several are now priced even higher.

Other French Art Deco poster artists worth looking for include Robert Bonfils, Jean Carlu, Paul Colin, Jean-Gabriel Domergue, Jean Dupas, Maurice Dufrène, Charles Gesmar, Georges Lepape and Charles Loupot.

Bonfils was a fashion illustrator who created one of the official posters for the 1925 Paris Exposition, with its leaping gazelle and stylized flowers, which now sells in its smaller 23" × 15" format for more than $3,000. (See "Recognizing Art Deco" for a photo of Bonfils's poster.)

Loupot was also a fashion designer, and he also designed a poster for the 1925 Exposition. With smoke rising from factories to create a giant rose in the sky, today it makes environmentalists cringe, but at the time it represented the marriage of industry and art, which was the overall Expo theme. Another fashion designer, Georges Lepape, best known for his fashion illustrations for *La Gazette du Bon Ton* and *Vogue*, also created several posters for clients such as the department store Galeries Lafayette and the Théâtre des Champs Élysées.

Jean Dupas was a fine artist who was drawn into the world of advertising through commissions by department stores. His distinctive style carried over into his advertising graphics. His poster for the Salon des Artistes Décorateurs, the influential circle of artists who controlled French design, and for the department store Arnold Constable are very desirable.

Jean Carlu was inspired by the Cubists. He was the creator of neon tube posters, both in three dimensions and as graphic designs, and did neon-inspired designs for the cover of *Vanity Fair*. He designed the poster for the 1937 Paris Exposition, as well as for everyday items such as toothpaste. Carlu's prices cover a broad range, with some still affordable and others selling for more than $10,000.

Many great posters were created for stage performers such as Josephine Baker, Mistinguett, and others. An artist called Zig (aka Louis Gaudin) created posters for both Baker and Mistinguett. Charles Gesmar, who designed about fifty posters in his short lifetime, created almost half of them for Mistinguett! However, the best-known and highest-priced Art Deco posters in this category are by Paul Colin.

In October, 2003, an incredibly rare collection of French Art Deco posters, assembled by a young French graphic designer, Jean Chassaing in the years between 1925 and 1932 came to the auction block at Swann Galleries in New York. Chassaing himself is almost unknown as a poster designer, in part because he appears to have been forced to look for other work in 1932 when the Depression took hold in Europe, and in part because he died at the young age of 33 in 1938. Evidence points to his work as an apprentice with Cassandre starting in 1925 and with Paul Colin starting in 1927. This young apprentice to the greats managed to collect and preserve some of the best examples of Art Deco posters, many never before seen.

At the Swann Galleries auction, the rare 1927 Colin poster for Josephine Baker's "Bal Nègre" at the Théâtre des Champs Élysées sold for $96,000, setting a new record for the artist, and a black-and-white proof of the same poster brought $23,000. The record did not stand long: two lots later in the same auction, the only known copy of Colin's 1929 poster for "La Revue Black Birds" at the Moulin Rouge sold for a staggering $167,500.

Other posters in the same sale sold for equally impressive figures, including a 1926 Cassandre poster for the department store Au Boucheron which was never before offered at auction, and sold for $50,600; Cassandre's 1925 "Cycles Brillant" at $34,500, and his 1929 "La Route Bleu," also at $34,500, setting new records for those posters at auction. Numerous other records were set, including one for Jean Chassaing's own 1931 poster of Josephine Baker, selling for $16,100, and the original *maquette* for the same poster bringing $9,200. In the end, Chassaing himself was elevated to a new position in the world of Art Deco posters.

Other European Art Deco Posters
Many other talented though lesser-known French designers created appealing Art Deco posters that are more affordable to collectors than those above. In addition, posterists in other European countries also produced outstanding Art Deco images.

The best Belgian Art Deco posterist, Leo Marfurt, created an advertising agency in 1927, Les Créations Publicitaires, which he ran until 1957. Like Cassandre's agency, Marfurt created posters for many clients, such as Belga Cigarettes, Chrysler and Minerva automobiles, the English LNER, resorts, and a host of others.

The best Dutch Art Deco posters were for products and travel. One notable designer is Wim ten Broek, whose posters for Holland-America Line ocean liners are reminiscent of A. M. Cassandre. Small wonder — Cassandre also designed posters for Holland-America and other Dutch companies. Other Dutch designers include Jan Wijga; notably his posters for KLM (Royal Dutch Airlines); and Johann von Stein for Lloyd Lines. Swiss artists Émile Cardinaux, Herbert Matter, and Otto Baumberger created some good Art Deco designs.

In England, the finest poster artist was an American, Edward McKnight Kauffer, known for his posters for the London Underground, English Rail, and Shell Oil, the three most important poster "patrons" in England. Perhaps his best known poster is "Power, The Nerve Center of the London Underground" (1930), depicting a man's fist emanating from a factory and train wheel, punctuated by zigzag lighting bolts. Other notable British artists include Austin Cooper, Charles Pears, Frank Newbould, Tom Purvis, and Fred Taylor.

Ludwig Hohlwein was the master of modern design in German posters, creating literally thousands of posters in his dramatic style and striking color combinations. His posters of animals, especially for the Munich Zoo,

are prized, and he was also skilled at film, travel, and advertising posters. Hans Rudi Erdt and Walter Schnackenberg also created some great Art Deco designs. While Schnakenberg's early, outstanding cabaret posters can sell for more than $20,000 at auction, perhaps the most sought-after German posters are for the 1927 Fritz Lang epic film *Metropolis*.

A poster by Werner Graul, 1926, for the first run of the film "Metropolis." Courtesy of Swann Galleries, NY.

This film, with its dark German Expressionist view of the vast futuristic city, has become an Art Deco icon. Four different posters for the film are known, but they are all extremely rare. In October, 2000, a 6' poster for the film realized an incredible $367,800 at auction. In May, 2003, at Swann Galleries, a much smaller 27" × 18" never-before-seen poster by Werner Graul for the first run of this film brought $41,400.

Italian Art Deco posters have been increasing in popularity recently. Many of the best Italian Art Deco posters are by Marcello. Another outstanding Italian artist, Severo

Pozzati, signed his works "Sepo." His product posters have been compared to those by Cassandre, and he in fact worked in France after 1920. The major figure in Italian poster design, Leonetto Cappiello, created some outstanding Art Deco images that are now highly sought-after. Cappiello's incredible lifetime output of more than 1,000 posters means that many good and better examples are still available for less than $3,000, while his best Art Deco posters command three times that amount.

American Posters

One might assume that the Modern style in the United States would yield a wealth of fine posters. However, in America, posters were a less effective advertising vehicle than magazines. In addition, American advertising used photographic images much earlier and, when illustrations were used, European designers were often commissioned to execute them.

One "American" posterist we proudly claim is Joseph Binder, an Austrian who worked extensively in Germany before coming to the U.S. Binder won the competition for poster design for the New York World's Fair of 1939. Ironically, another great collectible Art Deco American poster for the 1939 World's Fair is by Englishman John Atherton.

Binder did numerous posters before emigrating to the U.S., including a now well-known ski travel poster for Austria, published in several editions for global distribution, with the headline "Austria" in several languages. He also created covers for magazines such as *Fortune*.

American train posters from the 1920s to the 1940s are increasingly appearing on the poster market. Some of the best are by Leslie Ragan for the New York Central Railroad, depicting the skyscraper-studded skylines of the cities the trains served. Prices for Ragan's images have reached more than $4,000 at auction.

Other notable American travel poster artists who have drawn attention are Maurice Logan for Southern Pacific Railways; Sascha Maurer for the New Haven Railroad, and his outstanding ski posters for Flexible Flyer skis; Adolph Treidler for his posters for Bermuda and the New York Central Railroad; William Welsh for Pullman; and Gustav Krollman for Northern Pacific Railways.

These and other American travel posters of the period have surged both in popularity and price in recent years. Those depicting the famous Streamliner trains of the period, such as the Twentieth Century Limited, are the highest priced. Many better examples of these by other artists can still be purchased for less than $2,000, but they seem to be disappearing into private collections quickly, and there does not seem to be a depth of material available, increasing their prospects for appreciating quickly.

Pochoir Illustrations

Many French graphic artists began as fashion illustrators, rendering the fashion designs of Parisian *couturiers* such as Paul Poiret, Doeuillet, Paquin, Lanvin, and Worth, usually in gouache, an opaque paint mixed with water and applied like watercolors. The growth of fashion magazines allowed these designers to reach new audiences, and the development of *pochoir*, or stencil printing, in fashion magazines became popular.

In *pochoir* printing, the basic outline of the design was stenciled onto the page, and the colors were hand-applied. It could take more than two dozen women seated at long rows of tables over a week to hand-color all of the illustrations for a single issue of a magazine. This may sound laborious, but it produced a high-quality publication that suited the *de luxe* marketing of fashion.

These illustrations were published in numerous French magazines such as *Gazette du Bon Ton, Modes et Manières d'Aujoud'hui, Art, Goût et Beauté, Journal des Dames et des Modes, Falbalas et Fanfreluches, La Guirlande des Mois, Les Idées Nouvelles de la Mode*, and *Les Feuillets d'Art*. Some German magazines also used *pochoir* printing.

Better-known artists who created *pochoir* illustrations include George Barbier, Edouardo Benito, Paul Iribe, Georges Lepape, Charles Martin, Leon Bakst, André Marty and Pierre Brissaud.

Gazette du Bon Ton publisher Lucien Vogel brought the *pochoir* method to perfection, and illustrations from its 1912–1925 life tend to be the most valuable, with each illustration bringing anywhere from $100 to $300 or more depending on the quality of the illustration itself, the reputation of the graphic designer, and the reputation of the fashion designer whose work is depicted. The use of metallic inks or other elaborate hand-coloring adds to the value as well.

Thus, an illustration of a Cinderella gown by Doucet, executed by the well-known illustrator André Marty, or a Rodier "afternoon" dress illustrated by Georges Lepape, are twice as interesting for the collector.

However, *pochoirs* from many magazines can still be found at moderate prices and make wonderful Art Deco decorations. By the 1930s, *Art, Goût et Beauté* was the only fashion magazine still using *pochoir* hand-colored illustrations, and it stopped publication in 1932.

L'HEURE DU THÉ

Manteau de fourrure, de Jeanne Lanvin

Many of these same designers were also gifted book and portfolio illustrators. Several portfolios of *pochoirs* were designed during the early Art Deco period to illustrate legends, biographies of celebrities, or as portfolios that designers would show to their clients.

Plates by Edouard Benedictus from the portfolios "Variations," "Nouvelles Variations" and "Relais" (1930), which were created as designs for textiles, are also often found as individual pieces. Their strong design and color combinations make them decorative favorites, and they remain affordable, often retailing for $250 or less each plate.

The original gouaches or watercolors by these designers before they were rendered into *pochoir* prints are quite rare, and can be very expensive. Several original gouaches by Georges Lepape came up in 2001 at Doyle

New York and brought prices ranging from $700 for a small drawing to $16,000 for a gouache portrait of Nijinski in the Ballets Russes production of *Scheherazade*.

Magazine Covers

In America magazines were a more formidable advertising vehicle than posters, and cover graphics became an important means of selling a magazine at the newsstand. Originally rendered by the artist in watercolor, gouache, pen and ink, and other mediums, they were usually photo-mechanically reproduced.

Magazines which featured notable Art Deco covers include *Harper's Bazaar* (spelled "Bazar" until 1929); *Vanity Fair*; *Vogue*; *Woman's Home Companion*, especially covers by William Welsh; and *Fortune*. Some of the best covers are from a lesser-known magazine, *Asia*, which employed artist Frank McIntosh as art director from 1924 to about 1933.

Georges Lepape designed covers for *Femina*, *Modes et Manières d'Aujourd'hui*, *Art et Décoration*, and Lucien Vogel's *Gazette du Bon Ton*. He also designed for *Vanity Fair* starting in 1915 and for *Vogue* starting in 1916, both Condé Nast publications. His 114 covers for *Vogue*, created from 1916 to 1939, are highly prized. He had an eye for lettering, and changed the lettering of the magazine's name with each design. Today it is practically unthinkable that a magazine could compete on the stands if it changed its logo with every issue.

From 1915 to 1936, Erté designed 240 covers for *Harper's Bazaar*, which was the direct competitor of *Vogue*. His total illustrations, including numerous fashion layouts for various Hearst publications, may number closer to 2,500. Erté, whose real name is Romain de Tirtoff, emigrated to Paris from Russia, adopting his new name from the French pronunciation of his initials, "R.T."

Erté's original gouache fashion illustrations from the Art Deco period can sell for thousands of dollars, so paying in the range of $150 to $300 for a magazine in good condition sounds like a bargain. In many ways, these magazine covers are more truly Art Deco collectibles than his signed and numbered prints, the vast majority of which were published starting in 1974, right up to, and even

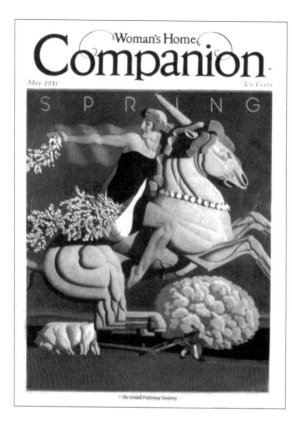

after his death in 1990. *Harper's Bazaar* covers by A. M. Cassandre are also highly collectible, though they appear somewhat more Surrealist than Deco in inspiration.

Vanity Fair employed a number of outstanding artists to design its covers, including Benito, Carlu, and George Bolin, whose 1920s Jazz Age themes reflect the impact of Cubism. Miguel Covarrubias's most famous cover for *Vanity Fair* is for the February, 1932, issue featuring Greta Garbo, whose pointed shoulders match her pointed eyebrows. In the 1930s *Vanity Fair* commissioned Frederick Chance and Paolo Garetto.

Fortune, which started one month after the Stock Market Crash of 1929, also featured modern idiom graphics and covers. Cover artists for *Fortune* include Cassandre, Joseph Binder, Antonio Petrucelli, Paolo Garetto, Fernand Leger, Ernest Hamlin Baker, Covarrubias, and others. *Fortune* magazine is a good source for covers in mint condition, because it came with a slipcase for storage. A great resource for *Fortune* collectors is the book *Fortune: The Art of Covering Business*, published in 1999 by Time, Inc., which depicts every cover from 1930 through 1950.

With relatively low prices, magazines are a popular Art Deco collectible, and one can still often find them in garage sales. However, the best Art Deco magazine covers in excellent condition are becoming harder to find, especially in urban markets, and dealers are more aware of their value than before. We recommend collecting the entire magazine wherever you can, and not just the detached cover—the contents, advertising, and articles inside are often a fascinating glimpse of the world when Art Deco reigned supreme. ◙

12
INDUSTRIAL DESIGN

The term "industrial designer" was coined by Norman Bel Geddes, who opened the first industrial design studio in America in 1927. From the late 1920s through the 1930s, several outstanding talents would distinguish themselves as designers for industry: Walter Dorwin Teague, Raymond Loewy, Donald Deskey, Kem Weber, Gilbert Rohde, Walter von Nessen, Viktor Schreckengost, Russel Wright and others. Many talented industrial designers also toiled anonymously for large corporations, and it is only today that some of their individual contributions are coming to light.

The early recognition of industrial design as a true "art" form came in 1934, when the New York Metropolitan

Museum of Art hosted the "Contemporary American Industrial Art" exhibition, and the Museum of Modern Art hosted its "Machine Art" exhibition.

The term "industrial design" can be used to describe a vast range of objects, if one defines it as "design for machine production." Much of the furniture, lighting, clocks, and even mesh purses and Bakelite jewelry are industrial design by this definition. It was only a matter of time before the machine itself became the object of machine design.

Some people use the term most often to apply to large-scale design for airplanes, ocean liners, dams, trains, and cars, especially since many of the designers of this era also designed for transportation. Major appliances, which do not yet figure greatly into the collecting market, also underwent industrial design changes in the 1920s and 1930s: refrigerators, stoves, washing machines, and oil burners. Today, however, collectors of industrial design tend to focus their attention on household appliances and office equipment: radios, telephones, irons, toasters, cameras, office machines, phonographs, and the like, all of which were redesigned to spur consumption during the Depression.

Streamlining became the overriding principle of industrial design. Speed, machine efficiency, and progress were the buzzwords of the day. Streamlining, which started with the new aerodynamic shapes of transportation vehicles to reduce resistance, is identified by its smooth, rounded surfaces and parabolic curves. One of the most frequent design motifs on Streamline consumer products are three horizontal or diagonal parallel lines that represented speed. When looking at industrial products, you'll notice that the logos of many corporations were "modernized" and applied to surfaces, becoming part of the overall design of the object.

The rediscovery of industrial design came much later than the resurgence of interest in Art Deco furnishings, decorative objects, or posters. It really wasn't until the groundbreaking 1986 exhibition "The Machine Age in America: 1914–1941" at the Brooklyn Museum that dealers and collectors started avidly seeking the best examples of the leading industrial designers of the period. Even

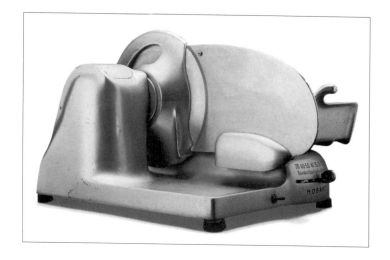

though it has matured rapidly in the years since that 1986 exhibition, there are still many discoveries to be made.

The problem is, a discovery made public can drive prices wild. Take for example the 1940 Art Deco "Streamliner" meat slicer designed by Egmont Arens and Theodore C. Brookhart. Savvy collector John C. Waddell bought one some time ago, and it was featured in the "American Modern" exhibition of his collection at the Metropolitan Museum of Art from May, 2000, to January, 2001. An overeager buyer snapped one up at Phillips, de Pury & Luxembourg in May, 2002, for $8,625. Maybe not that many people really need to own one of these, because the next time one came up, at Wright in Chicago in May, 2003, it only sold for $1,700.

In the late 1980s, industrial design was one of the hottest, trendiest areas for collecting. Prices on designs that could be attributed to leading designers shot up rapidly. At that time, the leading New York dealer in the field was Jacques Caussin, owner of First 1/2, who went on to produce Miami Modernism and other top 20th-century design shows across the country. When this author first interviewed him in 1987, his shop in SoHo was full of microphones, tools, an ElectroLux vacuum cleaner, and even a German lawnmower.

A favorite area for collectors is early electric appliances and equipment. While many of these today may seem

The 1940 "Streamliner" meat slicer by Arens and Brookhart. Courtesy of Phillips, de Pury & Luxembourg, NY.

old-fashioned or even rudimentary, they were the technological "modern living" breakthroughs of their day. The first AC plug-in radio was not manufactured until 1927, and by 1933 millions were tuning in to F.D.R.'s "Fireside Chats." In 1929 more than 600,000 refrigerators were sold in this country, but that number jumped to more than 1 million the following year. The goal of the industrial designer of the day was not to just make easier-to-produce, better-looking appliances, but to improve the product itself.

The November, 1934, issue of *Advertising Arts* magazine carried an article by Arthur Hirose entitled "Design in the Electrical Appliance Field," which underscored this point:

"Manufacturers, jobbers and retailers are looking for something that will make genuinely obsolete the appliances that long ago should have been retired. In many American homes today are toasters, percolators, vacuum cleaners, washers, waffle irons, heating pads, fans, lighting fixtures, and portable lamps that should be scrapped. Most of them still do the jobs poorly when contrasted with the newer developments of electrical appliance factories. Working together, electrical appliance makers and industrial designers can develop electrical appliances that will be profitable not only because these household devices look better but are better appliances."

New materials, treatments, finishes, and colors speeded the acceptance of household objects fashioned from plastics, chrome, and aluminum. The economic distress of the Depression was not reason enough to purchase a cocktail set in chrome instead of silver—it had to look good, too.

Manufacturers soon realized that a design- and fashion-conscious public would more readily buy an object if the designer's name was touted in product brochures, catalogues, and magazine advertisements: "the new washing machine designed by Lurelle Guild for the General Electric Company," "the new clock designed by Henry Dreyfuss for Seth Thomas,"...the list is almost endless. Soon the products themselves carried the designer's name: thus, Henry Dreyfuss's facsimile signature stamped in to the bottom of his now famous Thermos design. Russel Wright was the first designer to use his own name fully as a brand name—Martha Stewart, move over.

Dreyfuss's early career was in the theater, and he worked as an apprentice to Bel Geddes. He was only 25 in 1929 when he established his own industrial design firm in New York. Over the years he designed alarm clocks, pens and pencils, typewriters, telephones, and even farm equipment. He collaborated with designer Wallace Harrison to create "Democracity," the model city contained in the Perisphere at the 1939 World's Fair. He completely redesigned the New York Central Railroad's *Mercury* and the *20th Century Limited* Streamliner trains in 1936 and 1938, respectively.

Raymond Loewy, who immigrated from France after World War I, worked in the world of store window display at Saks Fifth Avenue and fashion illustration for *Vogue, Vanity Fair,* and other magazines. Like Dreyfuss, he opened his industrial design studio in 1929, and he too would eventually design a Streamliner for a railroad: Pennsylvania Railroad. Loewy also designed the "Hupmobile" (and later the "Avanti") car, and packaging for companies like Lucky Strike and Coca-Cola. He even designed the red Coca-Cola refrigerated machines, and went on much later to design a lunar landing module for NASA.

Dreyfuss and Loewy, along with Norman Bel Geddes and Walter Dorwin Teague, are considered the "big four" in industrial design of the period. Teague's "conversion" to industrial design and streamlining came suddenly in 1926 when he visited Europe and studied the work of Le Corbusier. Of all those named, he is the best known for design of household and everyday objects: cameras, lamps, radios, pens, and much more. Teague's 1930 Kodak Gift Camera has long been a highly collectible Art Deco icon.

Many industrial objects are hard to find in excellent condition: they were used every day, got banged or dented, and taken on journeys. In addition, when something "nice" owned by an aunt went out of fashion, she wasn't likely to throw it away—a vase, a Chanel dress, a table, a lamp. Instead, it was packed away in the attic, or given to

a child setting up their own apartment. The situation was different with most industrial design. When a clothing iron had outlived its usefulness, or an advanced model appeared, it wasn't enshrined with the family photos, it was thrown on the junk heap. Thus the rarity and high prices for some of the items in this field, which continues to attract attention as the collecting base slowly grows.

However, some items turned out to be less rare than was originally thought: for example, Teague's 1934 blue-mirrored Sparton "Bluebird" radios turned out to be plentiful. Perhaps because they were so attractive with the blue glass mirror, people didn't throw them out, so there was a dip in the market. One in good condition sold in May, 2003, at Ivey-Selkirk auctions for $3,450, up only slightly from ten years ago when it was selling in the $2,500 to $3,000 range.

In general the same is true of typical household appliances such as juicers, toasters, and irons. Though many are well-designed, they were not design breakthroughs, for the most part. They remain good examples of industrial design of the period, are still very affordable for the average collector, and they are just plain fun to have in the kitchen along with your Fiestaware!

In each category, though, a few outstanding designs have emerged that can command higher prices. Industrial design objects of this quality are also finding their way into American and foreign museums at an increasing rate.

Other industrial design items, such as Dreyfuss's Thermos and John Vassos's 1935 "RCA Victor Special"

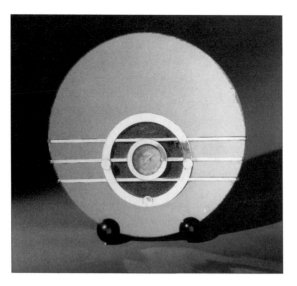

portable phonograph, have almost become icons of the era, and will no doubt continue to appreciate in value in the years ahead, although the rate of appreciation may be slower than was once thought. Recent retail listings offered a 6" Dreyfuss Thermos in teal for $395, and a 7" version in the same color for $595. A Vassos RCA Victor Special phonograph sold at a Wright auction in 2003 for $3,250, but ten years ago one sold for an almost equal amount at Skinner in Boston.

One of the consistently hottest industrial design collecting areas over the years has been Catalin radios. Catalin is not Bakelite. While both are trademarked names and nearly identical in chemical composition, Bakelite is usually found in only black, brown, and maroon, and was later manufactured in white and ivory. It has a dense, heavy appearance that rarely has any luster. Catalin, which is translucent, was cast as a liquid with a resin that could be clear, tinted to almost any color, or produced with eye-catching "marbleized" effects by mixing colors.

Not to confuse the issue further, but there were many other trade plastics that looked like Bakelite: Beetle, Durez, and others, as well as those that looked like Catalin: Marblette, Joanite, and Fiberlon. In addition, other plastics of different chemical composition were also widely in use. One example, celluloid, the oldest of

John Vassos'
1935 "RCA
Victor Special"
portable
phonograph.
Courtesy of
Skinner, Inc.,
Boston.

all plastics, was first produced around 1870 and was used into the 1920s for household and boudoir items.

Many of the best Catalin radios disappeared into private collections back in the 1980s, and it may be some time before we see those collections back on the market. Some rare Catalin radios sell for more than $10,000, and even those considered less scarce have climbed into the $3,000 to $5,000 range. For example, a Fada "Bullet" in blue marbled Catalin was recently listed with a retail price of $3,500. The less rare version in yellow with red trim listed for $1,650.

In actuality it turned out that relatively few Catalin radios survived, even though they were manufactured by about twenty American companies, such as General Electric Company, Emerson, Fada, Motorola, Bendix, and lesser-known firms. The first Catalin model did not appear until around 1935–1936, and just as they were gaining some real market popularity in 1939–1940, the war broke out, and production was suspended. Cases cracked, tubes burned holes in the plastic, radios warped in the sun or

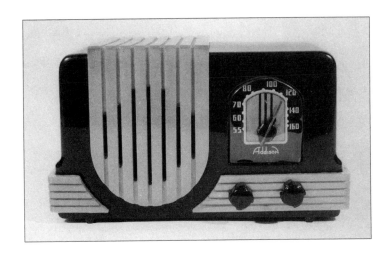

an overheated garage, and once they stopped working, even if the case was in good condition, few people kept them.

The collecting field got yet another boost with John Sideli's book *Classic Plastic Radios of the 1930s and 1940s* (E. P. Dutton, 1990), reinforcing the already high prices that were being paid. Of the fifty-four models listed in his book, at the time he considered twenty-four of them to be rare.

Collectors should beware that there are now reproductions on the market. What has emerged from the scarcity of Catalin radios is a growing interest in other models of radios from the 1930s and 1940s that still reflect the Art Deco style and that can be collected more affordably. Good and better examples of wood case radios with Art Deco styling can be purchased for $250 to $1,000. One of the best resources for learning more about the subject, as well as finding a number of items for sale, is Mark Stein's excellent books on tabletop radios and his Web site at *www.radiomania.com*. ◪

Addison radio, Model 2, 1940, in maroon and yellow Catalin. Author file photo. Courtesy of John Sideli.

13

ALL THAT GLITTERS: AN EPILOGUE

There are so many potential collecting areas in the world of Art Deco: hardly anything was untouched by this truly international design that invoked luxury, urban sophistication and, above all, style.

You might collect the metal mesh purses of Whiting & Davis, considered "the cat's pajamas" of flapper fashion, with their colorful geometric Art Deco patterns designed to dazzle. By 1928 mesh bags were so popular that the company operated 500 machines to stay ahead of the demand!

Or you could seek out the *dinanderie*, or designs on copper, of artists such as Camille Fauré, Claudius Linoissier, or from the French firm Christofle. Highly prized and highly priced, these hand-hammered, sometimes heavily enameled copper vases and decorations seem to scintillate in the light.

Fine Art Deco jewelry, by Cartier, Van Cleef and Arpels, and Mauboussin comes up in estate sales and attracts crowds at the Miami Beach Convention Center antique shows. America's oldest jewelry store, Black, Starr and Frost, also marketed Art Deco rarities. Listen closely to the words of the song "Diamonds are a Girl's Best Friend," and you'll hear their name.

In the 1930s, fashion designer Coco Chanel took the vogue for trendy jewelry to its logical conclusion: costume jewelry. The Depression brought Art Deco jewelry using marcasite, which is a name given to crystallized iron pyrite when it is set in silver. From a distance, a brooch set with hundreds of small marcasites appears to be shimmering with diamonds. Dazzling with the color of a Carmen Miranda headdress, Bakelite and Catalin jewelry has long been coveted by Art Deco mavens.

Hollywood memorabilia is a treasure trove of Art Deco "glitterati." Name your favorite Hollywood star from the 1920s and 1930s and it is quite possible you'll find their photo in a dazzling Art Deco glass and metal photo frame on the walls at Steve Starr Studios in Chicago. Starr's collecting passion, which started in 1976 and saw the publication of a book in 1991, has exploded into a display of more than 950 photo frames which cover every inch of the walls of his shop.

Picture frames of the Art Deco period can be found in Bakelite, celluloid, marble, wood, and other materials, and are often silk-screened in a variety of colors with geometric designs.

Sometimes the design on the glass was hand-engraved, hand-etched, or sandblasted, and some glass had scalloping or mirroring as well. Rare examples have cobalt blue or peach tinted glass.

Originally, many of these photo frames were sold with stock photos of the great actors and actresses at Paramount, Universal, Metro-Goldwyn-Mayer, 20th Century Fox, and other studios. Some retailed at finer stores such as Tiffany & Company and Marshall Field, and

Vintage photo of Mae West in an Art Deco photo frame. Courtesy of Steve Starr Studios, IL.

thousands were sold through W. T. Grant, Kresge's, and Woolworth's, with original prices as low as 10 cents.

High-style Art Deco souvenirs from the 1933 Chicago World's Fair," called "The Century of Progress," and the 1939 New York World's Fair, called "The World of Tomorrow" and other fairs of the era are eagerly snatched up in the marketplace. More than 50 million people attended the 1939 World's Fair, and estimates are that more than 25,000 different souvenirs were sold at the Fair. But by 1940 the Art Deco style was almost *too* stylish for a world faced with the horrors of war.

As lavish and star-struck as Hollywood, the great ocean liners of the period were veritable floating palaces of Art Deco. The French government commissioned the best Art Deco artists and artisans to design and outfit such liners as the *Normandie*, the *Île de France*, *L'Atlantique* and the *Paris*. One sought-after silver French Art Deco coffee service with ebony handles now being reproduced was designed by Christofle for the *Normandie*.

If you are lucky enough to ever visit the Carnegie Museum in Pittsburgh, you'll see the stunning "Chariot of Aurora," an 18' × 26' gilded and lacquered wall relief mural designed by Jean Dupas for the Grand Salon of the *Normandie*. Installed in the museum in 1998, it is one of the finest pieces of Art Deco in the country.

The Normandie made sixty-nine transatlantic crossings, arriving in New York Harbor in August, 1939, four days before Germany invaded Poland. It was requisitioned as a troop ship and stripped of her treasures, which went into storage. While being outfitted, a welder's torch set the liner ablaze and it capsized in the harbor, where it remained for a year before being cut up for scrap. Much like the Art Deco style itself, the panels were not rediscovered until the 1980s. ◨

14

THE INSTANT EXPERT QUIZ

1. What names are given to the three phases of evolution of the Art Deco style?

2. What was the name of the German design school which so greatly influenced the Modern style?

3. What was the leading design style at the turn of the century, before Art Deco?

4. What is an "ebeniste," and where does the word come from?

5. What was the powerful group to which many of the leading early French Art Deco designers belonged?

6. In 1929, what event emphasized the need for inexpensive mass-produced furniture?

7. Who was the early American Modernist whose bookcases resembled skyscrapers?

8. Which American designer coined the term "industrial design"?

9. What event in 1939 is considered the final culmination of the Art Deco style?

10. In addition to flowing water and bubbles, what other water image became an Art Deco design icon?

11. What event led to the influx of Egyptian motifs in Art Deco design more than any other?

12. What form of music is often identified with Art Deco motifs?

13. Which French designer is generally recognized as the leading early French Art Deco furniture designer?

14. Who was the leading designer of chryselephantine sculpture?

15. Which glass designer really got his start by making perfume bottles?

16. What was the name of the jazzy, angular line of glass created by Consolidated Glass?

17. Which British ceramic artist created a line of wares called "Bizarre?"

18. Which company is considered the leading American Art Deco ceramics manufacturer?

19. Which industrial designer designed the 20th Century Limited Streamliner train?

20. Who was the first designer to use his own name as a brand name?

Answers

1. French Art Deco, Modern, Streamline

2. The Bauhaus

3. Art Nouveau

4. An ebeniste is a cabinet maker, and the word comes from the wood ebony

5. Societé des Artistes Décorateurs

6. The stock market crash, leading to the Depression

7. Paul Frankl

8. Norman Bel Geddes

9. The New York World's Fair of 1939

10. The frozen fountain motif

11. The discovery of the tomb of King Tut in 1922

12. Jazz

13. Jacques-Emile Ruhlmann

14. Demetre H. Chiparus

15. Rene Lalique

16. Ruba Rombic

17. Clarice Cliff

18. Cowan Pottery

19. Henry Dreyfuss

20. Russel Wright

RESOURCE GUIDE

SELECTED AMERICAN ART DECO DEALERS

We have selected the following dealers for the quality of their merchandise, no matter what the price range, and for their integrity and professionalism.
• Denotes a dealer who specializes primarily in Mid-Century design but who also carries some Art Deco.

Antiquers III
Mark Feldman, Corey Warn
171A Harvard Street
Brookline, MA 02446
(617) 738-5555
Wed.–Sat. 11–4
American and European Art Deco, fine art, and French art glass.

Art Deco Collection.com
Richard Fishman
546 & 550 Grand Avenue
Oakland, CA 94610
(510) 465-1920
www.artdecocollection.com
Tues.–Fri. 12–7, Sat.–Sun. 12–5
20th-century furnishings, French and American.

Art Moderne
John Harmann, John Jung
P.O. Box 72
San Antonio, FL 33576
(352) 588-3437
Shows only. General line of Art Deco collectibles, decorative arts and prints.

• Arts 220
Fern Simon
895 1/2 Green Bay Road
Winnetka, IL 60093
(847) 501-3084
Tues.–Sat. 11–4 and by appointment

American and European 20th-century art and design.

• Avant Garde 1910–1950 Inc
Susan Cutler, Rose Dicarlo
1551 North Wells Street
Chicago, IL 60610
(312) 951-6681
www.avantgardeantiques.com
Tues.–Sat. 11–6, Sun. 12–5
Furnishings, glass, sculpture, and decorative arts, 1920s through 1950s.

Boss Fine Books
Thomas Boss
234 Clarendon Street, 4th Floor
Boston, MA 02116
(617) 421-1700
www.bossbooks.com
Tues.–Fri. 11–5:30; Sat. 12–5:30
"Art of the Book": illustration, cover design, fine bindings and fine printing, 1890-1940.

Calderwood Gallery
Gary & Janet Calderwood
1622 Spruce Street
Philadelphia, PA 19103
(215) 546-5357
www.calderwoodgallery.com
Tues.–Fri. 11–5:30; Sat. 12–5:30
Fine- to museum-quality French Art Deco, Modernist and 1940s furniture.

• Century Design Ltd.
David Deatheridge
6308 South Rosebury Avenue, Suite 3W
St. Louis, MO 63105
(314) 721-3719
www.centurydesignltd.com
Online and by appointment.
Vintage modern design with a focus on elegance.

• Cincinnati Modern
Alex Chronis
2929 Spring Grove Avenue
Cincinnati, OH 45225

(513) 708-7258
www.cmodern.com
Online and by appointment. Mid-Century furniture and lighting.

• Collage 20th Century Classics

Wlodek Makowanczyk, Abby
Makowanczyk
1300 North Industrial Boulevard
Dallas, TX 75207
(214) 828-9888
www.collageclassics.com
Mon.–Sat. 11–5
Architect-designed furniture and
decorative arts, 1920s–1980s.

Deco Doug

Doug Ramsey
106 West Fourth
Royal Oak, MI 48067
(248) 547-3330
Mon.–Sat. 12–6
Fine Art Deco barware, vintage
watches, industrial design, and objets d'art.

Deco-Dence

Justin Burgess, Mark McCay
3020 Canton Street
Dallas, TX 75226
(214) 744-3326
www.deco-dence.com
Online and by appointment
Vintage Modernist designs from
1920–1940; Italian Futurist furnishings; wide array of vintage cocktail
cabinets.

decodame.com/ Premier Designs

Lorial Francis, Bryan Francis
Naples, FL 34108
(239) 514-6797
www.decodame.com
Online and by appointment
Fine Art Deco through Mid-Century
Modern furniture, lighting, and decorative objects. Comprehensive design studio.

Decodence

Peter Linden, Eric Menard
1684 Market Street
San Francisco, CA 94102

(415) 553-4525.
www.decodence.com
Please call for hours.
High-quality decorative objects of
the 20th century, highlighting
French and American Art Deco.

Decorum

Jack Beeler
1400 Vallejo Street
San Francisco, CA 94109
(415) 474-6886
www.decorumsanfran.com
Tues.–Sat. 10:30–5:30 (please call
ahead)
French and American Art Deco objects, with emphasis on lamps and
lighting.

• designsmithgallery

David Smith
1342 Main Street
Cincinnati, OH 45202
(513) 421-1397
www.designsmithgallery.com.
By chance or by appointment; most
Fridays and Saturdays 12–6
Mid-Century furnishings and decorative arts.

Donzella LTD

Paolo Buffa
17 White Street
New York, NY 10013
(212) 965-8919
www.donzella.com
Mon.-Sat. 11–6
High-end furniture, lighting, objects,
and art of the 20th century.

Douglas Rosin Decorative Arts & Antiques,

Douglas Rosin, Gene Douglas
730 North Wells Street
Chicago, IL 60610
(312) 337-6556
www.douglasrosin.com
Tues.–Sat. 11–5:30 and by
appointment
An eclectic mix from the
1890s–1960s, where design is the
common denominator.

Dragonette Decorative Arts

Patrick J. Dragonette, Scott Roberts
750 North La Cienega Boulevard
Los Angeles, CA 90069
(310) 855-9091
Mon.–Fri. 10–6, Sat. 12–6
Specializing in Mid-Century design
circa 1920 to 1970.

E-modern

Chris Kennedy
P.O. Box 751
Northampton, MA 01061
(800) 366-3376
www.e-modern.net
Online and by appointment
Modern furniture and accessories,
1925–1975.

First 1/2

Jacques Caussin
P.O. Box 5030
Palm Springs, CA 92263-5030
(760) 322-1160
By appointment only
French Art Deco and American In-
dustrial Design, 1930s.

Fusco & Four

Tony Fusco, Robert Four
1 Murdock Terrace
Boston, MA, 02135
(617) 787-2637
www.ArtDecoNetwork.com
By appointment only.
As dealers, specializing in fine
prints, paintings, and sculpture,
1900–1950. Also offering consulting
and appraisal services for collectors,
corporations, and institutions.

• Good Design

Gail Garlick
New York, NY 10021
(212) 570-9914
www.gooddesignshop.com
Online and by appointment
20th-century Scandinavian, American, and Italian furniture and
decorative objects.

Historical Design Inc.

Daniel Morris, Denis Gallion
306 East 61st Street, 1st Floor West
New York, NY 10021
(212) 593-4528
www.historicaldesign.com
Mon.–Sat. 10–5
Specializing in avant-garde design
from 1880 through the entire 20th
century.

L.A. Moderne

Kim Veloso
947 North La Cienega Boulevard,
Suite A
Los Angeles, CA 90069
(310) 360-1656
www.lamoderne.com
Please call for hours
Quality furniture and accessories
from the first half of the 20th century.

La Rocco Galleries

Margartia and Catherine La Rocco
1010 Central Avenue
Naples, FL 34102
(239) 434-5678
www.laroccogalleries.com
Please call for hours
High-quality furniture and decorative objects, highlighting European
and American Art Deco.

La Verrerie D'Art

Alain Fournier, Cheryl Graeve
P.O. Box 757
Bowie, MD 20718
(301) 464-3251
www.decoesque.com
Online only
European art glass, ceramics, and
objects. Specializing in glass by
Charles Schneider.

• Lost City Arts

Jim Elkind
18 Cooper Square
New York, NY 10003
(212) 375-0500
www.lostcityarts.com
Mon.–Fri. 12–6, Sat.–Sun. 12–6.
Furniture, lighting, and accessories,
1920s-1960s.

Maison Gerard Ltd.

Gerard Widdershoven, Benoist Drut
53 East 10th Street

New York, NY 10003
(212) 674-7611
www.maisongerard.com
Mon.–Fri. 10–6
Specializing in fine- and museum-quality French Art Deco, 1920s–1940s.

Mode Moderne
Michael Glatfelder, Michael Wilson
159 North 3rd Street
Philadelphia, PA 19106
(215) 627-0299
www.modemoderne.com
Wed.–Sat. 12–6, Sun. 1–5
Furniture and furnishings from Art Deco, American Machine Age, and 1950s–1970s Modern.

Modern One
Benjamin Storck
7956 Beverly Boulevard
Los Angeles, CA 90048
(323) 651-5082
www.modern1.com
Mon.–Fri. 10–6
Specializing in high-style furniture by noted designers.

• Modern Times
Martha Torno, Tom Clark
1538 North Milwaukee Avenue
Chicago, IL 60622
(773) 772-8871
www.moderntimeschicago.com
Wed.–Fri. 1–6, Sat.–Sun. 12–6
Specializing in vintage Modern design in home furnishings, 1930s–1970s.

Modernage
Chuck Zuccarini, Kim Zuccarini
25 North Saginaw
Pontiac, MI 48342
(248) 745-0999
Wed.–Sat. 12–6
Furnishings, jewelry, and decorative arts from all 20th-century Modern movements.

Moderne Gallery
Robert Aibel
111 North Third Street
Philadelphia, PA 19106

(215) 923-8536
www.modernegallery.com
Tues.–Sat. 11–6
French and American Art Deco; plus Nakashima, Esherick, Maloof, and others of the American Craft Movement.

Modernism Gallery
Ric Emmett
1622 Ponce de León Boulevard
Coral Gables, FL 33134
(305) 442-8743
www.modernism.com
Mon.–Fri. 9–5, Sat. 12–5
French and American Art Deco furnishings, lighting, Posters, decorative arts, and fine art.

Mondo Cane
Greg Wootan, Patrick Parrish
143 West 22nd Street
New York, NY 10011
(212) 643-2274, (646) 486-7616
www.mondomodern.com
Mon.–Fri. 11–7, Sat. 12–6
American and European Modernist design, 1920–1960.

Greg Nanamura
Greg Nanamura
1202 Lexington Avenue
#222, New York, NY 10028
(917) 446-4170
www.gregnanamura.com
Mon.–Sat. 10–6
Avant-garde objects from Art Deco, Bauhaus, and other 20th-century design movements.

Off The Wall
Dennis Clark, Dennis & Lisa Boses
7325 Melrose Avenue
Los Angeles, CA 90046
(323) 930-1185
www.offthewallantiques.com
Please call for hours
Specializing in unique and eccentric 20th-century design.

John Prinster Art Deco & Moderne
John Prinster
3735 South Dixie Highway

West Palm Beach, FL 33405
(561) 835-1512
www.john-prinster.com
Tues.–Sat. 11–5
Furnishings, lighting, and decorative
arts by designers, 1920s–1940s.

Frank Rogin 20th Century Objects of Art & Design
Frank Rogin
21 Mercer Street, 5th Floor
New York, NY 10013
(212) 431-6545
www.rogin.com
Mon.–Fri. 12–6 and by appointment
European furniture and lighting
from 1900–1960.

• Route 66
Matt Burkholz
14 Main Street
Chatham, NY 12037
(518) 392-6878
Seasonal (generally Thurs.–Sun. 11–5)
Specializing in jewelry: Bakelite, vintage designer costume, Mexican
and modern silver, and more.

Skyscraper
Sandi Berman
237 East 60th Street
New York, NY 10022
(212) 588-0644
www.skyscraperny.com
Mon.–Fri. 10–6, Sat. by appointment
Fine European and American furniture, art, and objects, 1930s–1940s.

Sparkle Plenty
Elizabeth Chadis
Newton, MA 02460
(617) 969-1193
By appointment only
Vintage costume jewelry: Bakelite,
Miriam Haskell, Chanel, Trifari, and
others.

• Springdale
Jim Toler
19 South Elm Street
Three Oaks, MI 49128
(269) 756-9896

www.springdalefurnishings.com
Specializing in vintage Heywood-Wakefield, with other Modernist and
Deco furniture.

Steve Starr Studios
Steve Starr
2779 North Lincoln Avenue
Chicago, IL 60614
(773) 525-6530
Mon.–Thurs. 2–6, Fri. 2–5,
Sat.–Sun. 1–5 or by appointment
Specializing in Art Deco photo
frames and furnishings.

• Try to Remember
Ira Raskin
5120 Wilson Lane
Bethesda, MD 20814
(301) 652-1695
9–5 daily, closed Wed
20th-century functional nostalgia:
lamps, books, jewelry, clocks, prints,
and furniture.

20th Century Provenance
Angelo Masaracchio, Rick Sementa
348 Broadway
Cambridge, MA 02139
(617) 547-2300
www.20thcenturyprovenance.com
Wed.–Sun. 12–5
20th-century furniture and accessories, specializing in Art Deco.

• Vertu
Roger Ellingsworth, Robert Rozycki
514 South Washington
Royal Oak, MI 48067
(248) 545-6050
Mon.–Sat. 11–5 or by appointment
Art Deco, Machine Age, and Mid-Century designer furnishings and
decorative arts.

Zig Zag
Marsha Evaskus
3419 North Lincoln Avenue
Chicago, IL 60657
(773) 525-1060
Wed.–Fri. 2–6, Sat. 1–6, Sun. 1–4
Art Deco and Moderne,
1920s–1940s objects, furniture, and
jewelry, industrial design, and more.

INTERNATIONAL ART DECO SOCIETIES

The following organizations are all sponsors of the International Coalition of Art Deco Societies (ICADS). We encourage you to join one or more of the following groups to further your appreciation of Art Deco and to help ensure its worldwide preservation

Australia
Melbourne
Art Deco Society Inc.
P.O. Box 17
Camberwell, VIC 3124
Australia
(61) 3 9183 4365
www.artdeco.org.au
Robin Grow, President

Perth
Art Deco Society of Western Australia
The Old Observatory
West Perth, WA 6005
Australia.
(61) 3 9321 6634
Vyonne Geneve, President

Sydney
Art Deco Society of NSW
P.O. Box 752
Willoughby, NSW 2068
Australia
(61) 2 9319 1125
www.welcome.to/artdeconsw
Jennifer Hill, President

Sydney
20th Century Heritage Society of NSW
P.O. Box Q1072
QVB Post Office
Sydney, NSW 1230
Australia
(61) 2 9878 2521
www.twentieth.org.au
Roy Lumby, Chairman.

Canada
Montréal
Art Deco Society of Montreal
3778 Chemin de la Côte-des-Neiges
Montréal, QC, H3H 1V6
Canada
(514) 931 9325
www.artdecomontreal.com
Sandra Rose, President

Toronto
Art Deco Society of Toronto
216 Carlton Street
Toronto, ON, M5A 2LI
Canada
www.artdecotoronto.com
Tim Morawetz and Dr. Ken Lipinski, Co-Founders.

Vancouver
Canadian Art Deco Society
#1030-470 Granville Street
Vancouver, BC, V6C 1V5
Canada.
Donald Luxton, President
(604)688 1216.

New Zealand
Auckland
Art Deco Society of Auckland
P.O. Box 109-304
Auckland, New Zealand
Betty Bayley, President
(64) 9 620 7484
www.artdeco.org.nz

Napier
Art Deco Trust
P.O. Box 133
Napier, New Zealand
Robert McGregor, Executive Director
(64) 6 835 0022
www.artdeconapier.com

South Africa
Cape Town
Cape Art Deco Society
P.O. Box 101
Piketberg, 7320
South Africa
Brent Meersman, Chairman

Durban
Durban Art Deco Society
14 Lawrence Road
Durban, 4001
South Africa
Dennis J. Claude, President

United Kingdom
London
Twentieth Century Society
70 Cowcross Street
London, EC1M 6EJ
United Kingdom
Catherine Croft, Director
(44) 20 7250 3857
www.c20society.demon.co.uk

United States
Boston
Art Deco Society of Boston
1 Murdock Terrace
Brighton, MA 02135
Tony Fusco, President
(617) 787 2637.

Chicago
Chicago Art Deco Society
P.O. Box 1116, Evanston, IL
60204-1116
Bennett Johnson, President
(847) 869-5059
www.chicagoartdecosociety.com

Dallas
Friends of Fair Park
1121 1st Avenue, Dallas, TX 75210
Craig Holcomb, Executive Director
(214) 426-3400

Detroit
Detroit Area Deco Society
P.O. Box 1393
Royal Oak, MI 48068-1393
Robin Cohen, President
(248) 582-3326
www.daads.org

Los Angeles
Art Deco Society of Los Angeles
P.O. Box 972
Hollywood, CA 90078
Mitzi March Mogul, President

(310) 659-3326
www.adsla.org

Miami Beach
Miami Design Preservation League
P.O. Box 190180, Miami Beach, FL
33119
Michael Kinerk, Board Chair
(305) 672-2014
ww.mdpl.org

New York
Art Deco Society of New York
P.O. Box 160
Planetarium Station
New York, NY 10024
Kathryn Hausman, President
(212) 679-DECO
www.artdeco.org

Olympia, Washington
Art Deco Society Northwest
1216 Devon Loop NE
Olympia, WA 98505
Joyce Colton, President
(360) 357 9408
www.artdeconw.org

Palm Beach, Florida
Art Deco Society of the Palm
Beaches
325 SW 29th Avenue
Delray Beach, FL 33445
Sharon Koskoff, President
(561) 276-9925

Sacramento
Sacramento Art Deco Society
P.O. Box 162836
Sacramento, CA 95816-2836
Doreen Sinclair, President
(916) 863-9667
www.sacdeco.org

San Francisco
Art Deco Society of California
100 Bush Street, Suite 511
San Francisco, CA 94104
Cherie Morrison Oliver, President
(415) 982-4094
www.art-deco.org

Tulsa
Tulsa Art Deco Society
2926 E. 39th Street

Tulsa, OK 74105-3704
Rex Ball, President
(918) 748-9188
www.tulsahistory.org

Washington, D.C.
Art Deco Society of Washington
P.O. Box 42722
Washington, DC 20015-2722
Jonathan Mazur, President
(202) 298-1100
www.adsw.org

SELECTED AMERICAN MUSEUMS WITH SIGNIFICANT COLLECTIONS OF ART DECO OR MODERNISM

Many American museums now have collections of Art Deco and other 20th-century design movements. The following general and specialized museums have significant collections or particularly outstanding holdings

Art Institute of Chicago
111 South Michigan Avenue
Chicago, IL 60603
(312) 443-3600
www.artic.edu

The Brooklyn Museum
200 Eastern Parkway
Brooklyn, NY 11238
(718) 638-5000
www.brooklynart.org

Carnegie Museum of Art
4400 Forbes Avenue
Pittsburgh, PA 15213
(412) 622-3131
www.cmoa.org

Cleveland Museum of Art
11150 East Boulevard, Cleveland,
OH 44106. (888) CMA-0033
www.clevelandart.org

Cooper-Hewitt Museum
2 East 91st Street
New York, NY 10128
(212) 860-6868
www.ndm.si.edu

The Corning Museum of Glass
1 Museum Way
Corning, NY 14830
(607) 937-5371
www.cmog.org

Cowan Pottery Museum (of Rocky River Public Library)
1600 Hampton Road
Rocky River, OH 44107
(216) 333-7610
www.rrpl.org/rrpl_cowan.stm

Cranbrook Academy of Art Museum
39221 Woodward Avenue
P.O. Box 801
Bloomfield Hills, MI 48303
(248) 645-3361.
www.cranbrook.edu/art/museum/

Everson Museum of Art
401 Harrison Street
Syracuse, NY 13202
(315) 475-6064
www.fmhs.cnyric.org/community/everson/

Metropolitan Museum of Art
1000 Fifth Avenue
New York, NY 10028
(212) 535-7710
www.metmuseum.org

Minneapolis Institute of Arts
2400 Third Avenue South
Minneapolis, MN 55404
(612) 870-3131
www.artsmia.org

Newark Museum
49 Washington Street
Newark, NJ 07102
(973) 596-6550
www.newarkmuseum.org

The Skyscraper Museum
5 East 22nd Street
Suite 30P
New York, NY 10010

(212) 766-1324
www.skyscraper.org

Virginia Museum of Fine Arts,
2800 Grove Avenue
Richmond, VA 23221
(804) 340-1400
www.vmfa.state.va.us

Walter Gropius House, a property of the Society for the Preservation of New England Antiques (SPNEA)
68 Baker Bridge Road
Lincoln, MA 01773
(617) 227-3956
wwww.spnea.org

The Wolfsonian-Florida International University
1001 Washington Avenue
Miami Beach, FL 33139
(305) 531-1001
www.wolfsonian.fiu.edu

CALENDAR OF U.S. ART DECO AND MODERNISM SHOWS

Note: We have placed these shows in the months that they generally happen, but dates can vary. It's best to check with the show to be sure of the exact dates.

January
Miami Modernism
Jaques Caussin and Dolphin Productions
P. O. Box 7320
Fort Lauderdale, FL 33338
(954) 563-6747
www.antiqnet.com/dolphin

February
Palm Springs Modernism
Jaques Caussin and Dolphin Productions
P. O. Box 7320

Fort Lauderdale, FL 33338
(954) 563-6747
www.antiqnet.com/dolphin

March
20th Century Cincinnati
Queen City Shows
Bruce Metzger
P.O. Box 35
Shandon, OH 45063
(513) 738-7256
www.20thcenturycincinnati.com

Triple Pier Antiques Show
Pier 88
Stella Show Management
151 West 25th Street, Suite 2
New York, NY 10001
(212) 255-0020
www.stellashows.com

April
Michigan Modernism
M & M Enterprises
19946 Great Oaks Circle South
Clinton Township, MI 48036
(586) 469-1706.
www.antiqnet.com/M&M

Chicago Modernism
Jaques Caussin and Dolphin Productions
P. O. Box 7320
Fort Lauderdale, FL 33338
(954) 563-6747
www.antiqnet.com/dolphin

May
LA Modernism
Dennis and Lisa Boses
7325 Melrose Avenue
Los Angeles, CA 90046
(818) 244-1126
www.lamodernism.com

June
Art Deco to 60's Sale
Peter and Deborah Kerestury
1217 Waterview Drive
Mill Valley, CA 94941
(650) 599-DECO
www.artdecosale.com

Exposition of the Decorative Arts
Art Deco Society of Washington, D.C.
P.O. Box 42722
Washington, DC 20015
(202) 298-1100
www.adsw.org

September
The International Art & Design Fair
at the New York Park Avenue Armory
Haughton International Fairs
31 Old Burlington Street
London, England W1S 3AS
(44) 0-20-7734-5491
www.haughton.com

October
The Modern Show
Stella Show Management
151 West 25th Street
Suite 2
New York, NY 10001
(212) 255-0020
www.stellashows.com

Modern Times
Tauni Brown
P. O. Box 342
Topanga, CA 90290
(310) 455-2894
www.moderntimesla.com

November
Triple Pier Antiques Show
Pier 88
Stella Show Management
151 West 25th Street
Suite 2
New York, NY 10001
(212) 255-0020
www.stellashows.com

Winnetka Modernism
Winnetka Community House
620 Lincoln Avenue
Winnetka, IL 60093
(847) 446-0537
www.winnetkacommunityhouse.org

Modernism: A Century of Art & Design
Sanford Smith Associates
68 East 7th Street
New York, NY 10003
(212) 777-5218
www.sanfordsmith.com

December
Art Deco to 60's Sale
Peter and Deborah Kerestury
1217 Waterview Drive
Mill Valley, CA 94941
(650) 599-DECO
www.artdecosale.com

AMERICAN AUCTION HOUSES HOSTING REGULAR DEDICATED AUCTIONS OF ART DECO OR MODERNIST DESIGN

Bonhams & Butterfields
20th Century Department
220 San Bruno Avenue
San Francisco, CA 94103
(415) 861-7500
www.bonhams.com/us

Christie's New York
Redway Nicola
20 Rockefeller Plaza
New York, NY 10020
(212) 636-2240
www.christies.com

David Rago Auctions
David Rago, John Sollo
333 North Main St.
Lambertville, NJ 08530
(609) 397-9374
www.ragoarts.com

Doyle New York
Reid Dunavant
175 East 87th Street
New York, NY 10128
(212) 427-2730
www.doylenewyork.com

Ivey-Selkirk Auctioneers
Mark O. Howald
7447 Forsyth Boulevard
St. Louis, MI 63105
(314) 726-5515
www.iveyselkirk.com

Los Angeles Modern Auctions
Peter Loughrey
P.O. Box 462006
Los Angeles, CA 90046
(323) 904-1950
www.lamodern.com

Phillips, de Pury & Luxembourg
Philippe Garner
450 West 15th Street
New York, NY 10011
(212) 940-1268
www.phillips-dpl.com

Skinner
Jane Prentiss
357 Main Street
Bolton, MA 01740
(978) 779-6241
www.skinnerinc.com

Sotheby's New York
James Zematis
1334 York Avenue
New York, NY 10021
(212) 606 7414
www.sothebys.com

Swann Galleries
Nicholas Lowry
104 East 25th Street
New York, NY 10010
(212) 254-4710
www.swanngalleries.com

Treadway Gallery
Don Treadway
2029 Madison Road
Cincinnati, OH 45208
(513) 321-6742
www.treadwaygallery.com

Wright
Richard Wright
1140 West Fulton
Chicago, IL 60607
(312) 563-0020.
www.wright20.com

BIBLIOGRAPHY

Museum Exhibition Catalogs or Accompanying Books

Often the best and most thoroughly researched books are those published in conjunction with museums and exhibitions. Those below are particularly sought after references for Art Deco enthusiasts. While many of the earlier works are out of print, they are worth finding as collectibles in their own right.

1925. *Encyclopédie des Arts Industriels et Modernes au XXème Siecle*. Imprimeries Nationale. Twelve volumes covering the groundbreaking 1925 Paris Exposition in detail. Reprinted in French. New York: Garland Publishers, 1977.

1929. *The Architect and the Industrial Arts*. New York: Metropolitan Museum of Art. The first exhibition in America reflecting Modern design.

1934. *Machine Art*. New York: Museum of Modern Art. The seminal exhibition that marked the true coming of age of the Industrial Designer.

1966. *Les Années 1925*. Catalogue by Yvonne Brunhammer. Two volumes. Musée des Arts Decoratifs, Paris. The first major retrospective exhibition in France focusing on the 1925 Exposition, which spurred the revival of interest in Art Deco.

1970. *Art Deco*. Catalogue by Judith Applegate. Finch College Museum of Art, New York. The first retrospective exhibition in the United States.

1971. *The World of Art Deco*. Catalogue by Bevis Hillier. Minneapolis Institute of Arts, Minneapolis. New York: E. P. Dutton, 1971. The first major retrospective exhibition in the United States, which incorporated the earlier Finch College exhibition.

1979. *Thirties*. Catalogue by the Arts Council of Great Britain. Hayward Gallery, Victoria and Albert Museum, London. The first major retrospective exhibition in England focusing on all aspects of the 1930s.

1983. *At Home in Manhattan: Modern Decorative Arts, 1925 to the Depression*. Catalogue by Karen Davies. New Haven, CT: Yale University Art Gallery.

1983. *Design in America: The Cranbrook Vision 1925–1950*. New York: Harry N. Abrams, Inc. In association with the Detroit Institute of Arts and the Metropolitan Museum of Art. An exhibition which focused on the important design influence of the Cranbrook Academy.

1985. *High Styles: Twentieth Century Design*. New York: Whitney Museum of American Art in association with Summit Books.

1986. *Vienna 1900*. Catalogue by Kirk Varnedoe. New York: The Museum of Modern Art. A groundbreaking exhibition emphasizing the Viennese Secession as an early modern design movement.

1986. *The Machine Age in America*. Book by Richard Guy Wilson, Diane H. Pilgrim, and Dickran Tashjian. New York: The Brooklyn Museum in association with Harry N. Abrams. A seminal exhibition focusing on American industrial design.

1987. *The Art That is Life: The Arts and Crafts Movement in America, 1875–1920*. Book by Wendy Kaplan. Boston: Little, Brown and Company, for the Museum of Fine Arts. A major retrospective on the Arts and Crafts movement which evidenced its impact on modern design.

1987. *American Art Deco*. Book by Alastair Duncan. Renwick Gallery, Smithsonian Institute, Washington, D.C., in association with New York: Harry N. Abrams. The first major exhibition to focus entirely on American Art Deco design.

1987. *Bentwood and Metal Furniture*. Book by Derek Ostergard et al., in conjunction with the exhibition at the American Federation of Arts, New York.

1989 *Art Déco en Europe*. Palais des Beaux-Arts, Brussels, Belgium. Catalogue edited by the Société des Expositions. An important retrospective on European Art Deco.

1990. *High & Low: Modern Art/Popular Culture*. Book by Kurt Varnedoe and Adam Gropnik. NY: Museum of Modern Art. Not specifically Art Deco, but an important exhibition for its focus on "low" culture: comics, advertising, graffiti, and more.

1991. *The 1920s: Age of the Metropolis*. Edited by Jean Clair. Montreal: Montreal Museum of Fine Arts. An important retrospective on the 1920s in fine and decorative arts.

1991. *Design 1935–1965: What Modern Was*. IBM Gallery, New York City from the collection of the Montreal Museum of Decorative Arts. Book edited by Martin Eidelberg. New York: Harry N. Abrams. An important exhibition and sourcebook on modern design from the end of the Art Deco period through the mid-1960s.

1993. *Industrial Design: Reflection of a Century*. Flammarion/APCI, Paris, 1993, in conjunction with the exhibition at the Grand Palais, Paris.

1995. *Designing Modernity: The Arts of Reform and Persuasion,*

1885–1945. Selections from the Wolfsonian collection, Miami Beach, FL. Kaplan, Wendy, ed. London: Thames and Hudson. The inaugural exhibition of this internationally important museum founded by Mitchell Wolfson.

1997. *Designed for Delight*. Eidelberg, Martin Ed. Quebec: Flammarion, 1997. In conjunction with the exhibition at the Montreal Museum of Art.

1998. *Modernism, 1880–1940, Masterworks from the Norwest Collection*. Kimbell Art Museum, Fort Worth, Texas. Book by Alastair Duncan. Wappinger's Falls, NY: Antique Collector's Club.

2000. *American Modern, 1925–1940: Design for a New Age*. Johnson, J. Stewart, New York: Harry N. Abrams. In conjunction with the Metropolitan Museum of Art exhibition of the same name, featuring the collection of John C. Waddell.

2003. *Art Deco: 1910–1939*. Benton, Charlotte Ed., Tim Benton, and Ghislaine Wood. New York: Bullfinch Press. In conjunction with the Victoria & Albert Museum exhibition of the same name, the first major museum retrospective in more than 15 years.

Victoria & Albert Museum, London: March 27, 2003–July 20, 2003

Royal Ontario Museum, Toronto: Sept. 20, 2003–January 4, 2004

Fine Arts Museum of San Francisco March 13, 2004–July 5, 2004 Museum of Fine Arts, Boston August 22, 2004–January 9, 2005

Overviews on Art Deco and Collecting Guides

There are hundreds of books on Art Deco. Below we try to select some of the best and most useful as well as those which you are more likely to find in print, and those most recently published. We apologize to the many gifted authors whose books we did not have room to mention.

Arwas, Victor. *Art Deco*. London: Academy Editions, 1975. Revised Editions: New York: Harry N. Abrams, 1992, 2000.

Brunhammer, Yvonne and Tise, Suzanne. *The Decorative Arts of France: La Société des Artistes Décorateurs 1900–1942*. New York: Rizzoli International, 1990.

Fusco, Tony. *The Confident Collector Identification and Price Guide to Art Deco*, 2nd Edition. New York: Ballantine, 1993.

Gallagher, Fiona Ed. *Christie's Art Deco*. New York: Watson-Guptill Publications, 2000.

Gaston, Mary Frank. *Collectors Guide to Art Deco*. Kentucky: Collector Books, 1989, revised 2000.

Hillier, Bevis. *Art Deco*. London: The Herbert Press, 1968 and New York: Schocken Books, 1985. The book that coined the term "Art Deco."

Hillier, Bevis and Stephen Escritt. *Art Deco Style*. Boston: Phaidon Press, 2003.

Klein, Dan; McClelland, Nancy A.; and Haslam, Malcolm. *In the Deco Style*. New York: Rizzoli International, Inc, 1986, republished 2002.

Knowles, Eric. *Miller's Art Deco (Miller's Antiques Checklist)*. London: Mitchell Beazley, 2001.

Ostergard, Derek E. *Art Deco Masterpieces*. New York: Hugh Lauter Levin, 1991.

Wood, Ghislaine. *Essential Art Deco*. New York: Bullfinch Press, 2003.

Architecture and Preservation

Bayer, Patricia. *Art Deco Architecture: Design, Decoration and Detail from the Twenties and Thirties*. New York: Harry N. Abrams, 1992. Republished: London: Thames & Hudson, 1999.

Gebhard, David. *The National Trust Guide to Art Deco in America*. Collingdale, PA: Diane Publishing, 1996.

Kinerk, Michael and Wilhelm, Dennis. *Rediscovering Art Deco U.S.A.* New York: E.P. Dutton, 1993.

Furnishings, Interiors and Specific Designers

Adam, Peter. *Eileen Gray: Architect/Designer: A Biography*. New York, Harry N. Abrams, 1987. Republished: New York: Acanthus Press, 2001.

Adams, Henry. *Viktor Schreckengost and 20th Century Design*. Cleveland: The Cleveland Museum of Art, 2000. In conjunction with the museum exhibition of the same name.

Albrecht, Donald, et al. *Russel Wright: Creating American Lifestyle*. New York: Harry N. Abrams, 2001. In conjunction with the exhibition by the same name at the Cooper-Hewitt National Design Museum.

Bayer, Patricia. *Art Deco Interiors*. Boston: Bullfinch Press, Little, Brown & Co., 1990. Republished: London: Thames & Hudson, 1998.

Camard, Florence. *Ruhlmann, Master of Art Deco*. New York: Harry N. Abrams, Inc., 1984.

Day, Susan. *Art Deco and Modernist Carpets*. San Francisco: Chronicle Books, 2002.

Duncan, Alastair. *Art Deco Furniture: The French Designers*. New York: Holt, Reinhart and Winston, 1984. Republished: London: Thames & Hudson, 1997.

Hardy, Alain-René. *Art Deco Textiles: The French Designers*. London: Thames & Hudson, 2003.

Hillman, Herb. *Art Deco Lighting*. Atglen: Schiffer Publishing, 2001.

Kahr, Joan. *Edgar Brandt: Master of Art Deco Ironwork*. New York: Harry N. Abrams, 1999.

Samuels, Charlotte. *Art Deco Textiles*. London: Victoria & Albert Museum, 2003.

Stein, Mark V. *20th Century Modern Clocks: Desk, Shelf and Decorative*. Baltimore: Radiomania Books, 2001.

Sculpture

Arwas, Victor. *Art Deco Sculpture: Chryselephantine Statuettes of the Twenties and Thirties*. London: Academy Editions and St. Martin's Press, New York, 1975.

Shayo, Alberto. *Chiparus: Master of Art Deco*. New York: Abbeville Press, 1999.

Glass

Arwas, Victor. *Glass: Art Nouveau to Art Deco*. London: Academy Editions and New York: Rizzoli International, 1977. Republished, expanded edition, New York: Harry N. Abrams, 1987, 1999.

Charleston, Robert J. *Masterpieces of Glass: A World History from the Corning Museum of Glass*. New York: Harry N. Abrams, 1990.

Dawes, Nicholas M. *Lalique: A Century of Glass for a Modern World*. 1989, Fashion Institute of Technology, New York. Catalogue for the first comprehensive survey/exhibition since 1933.

Duncan, Alastair. *Orrefors Glass*. New York: Antique Collectors Club, 1996.

Ericsson, Anne-Marie, et al. *The Brilliance of Swedish Glass, 1918–1939*. Yale University Press, 1996, in conjunction with the exhibition.

McClinton, Katherine Morrison. *Introduction to Lalique Glass*. Des Moines: Wallace-Homestead, 1978.

Pina, Leslie et al. *Depression Era Art Deco Glass*. Atglen, PA: Schiffer Publishing, 1999.

Wilson, Jack D. *Phoenix and Consolidated Art Glass 1926–1980*. Marietta, Ohio: Antique Publications, 1989.

Ceramics

Ball, Gregory, Editor. *Catteau*. Brussels, Belgium: King Baudouin Foundation, 2001, English translation, the collection of Claire De Pauw & Marcel Stal donated to the Belgian government. The only book currently available in English on Boch Frères.

King Bassett, Mark and Victoria Naumann. *Cowan Pottery and the Cleveland School*. Atglen, PA: Schiffer Publishing, 1998.

Chipman, Jack. *Collector's Encyclopedia of California Pottery*. Paducah, KY: Collector Books, 1991.

Cunningham, Helen C. *Clarice Cliff & Her Contemporaries*. Atglen, PA: Schiffer Publishing, 1999.

Eatwell, Ann Ed. and Andrew Casey Ed. *Susie Cooper: A Pioneer of Modern Design*. Wappinger's Falls, NY: Antique Collector's Club, 2003.

Griffin, Leonard. *Clarice Cliff: The Art of the Bizarre*. N. Pomfret, VT: Trafalgar Square Publishing, 1999.

McCready, Karen. *Art Deco and Modernist Ceramics*. London: Thames & Hudson, 1995.

Reiss, Ray. *Red Wing Art Pottery*. Chicago: Property Publishing, 1996.

Serpell, David. *Collecting Carlton Ware*. Iola, WI: Krause Publications, 1999.

Spours, Judy. *Art Deco Tableware*. New York: Rizzoli International, 1988.

Silver, Chrome & Cocktails

Johnson, Donald-Brian and Pina, Leslie. *Chase Complete: Deco Specialties of the Chase Brass & Copper Co.* Atglen, PA: Schiffer Publishing, 1999.

Johnson, Donald-Brian and Pina, Leslie. *Art Deco Lighting by Chase*. Atglen, PA: Schiffer Publishing, 2000.

Johnson, Donald-Brian and Pina, Leslie. *Chase Catalogs: 1934 and 1935: Chromium Brass and Copper Specialties*. Atglen, PA: Schiffer Publishing, 1998, and *The Chase Era: 1933 & 1942 Catalogs of the Chase Brass & Copper Co*. Atglen, PA: Schiffer Publishing, 2000.

Krekel-Aalberse, Annelies. *Art Nouveau, Art Deco Silver*. London: Thames and Hudson Ltd., 1989.

Venable, Charles, et al. *Silver in America 1840–1940: A Century of Splendor*. New York: Harry N. Abrams, 1995.

Visakay, Stephen. *Vintage Bar Ware Identification and Value Guide*. Paducah, KY: Collector Books, 1997.

Posters and Graphics

Ades, Dawn. *Twentieth Century Poster-Design of the Avant Garde*. Walker Art Center, in association with New York: Abbeville Press, 1984.

Bartha, Georges de and Duncan, Alastair. *Art Nouveau and Art Deco Bookbinding*. New York: Harry N. Abrams, 1989.

Fusco, Tony. *The Official Identification and Price Guide to Posters*, 2nd Edition. New York: New York: Ballantine, 1994.

Kery, Patricia Frantz. *Art Deco Graphics*. New York: Harry N. Abrams, 1986. (The definitive resource and still in print.)

Warshaw Berman, Susan. *Affordable Art Deco Graphics*. Atglen: Schiffer Publishing, 2002.

Wrede, Stuart. *The Modern Poster*, 1988. Museum of Modern Art, New York. New York: Museum of Modern Art in association with Boston: Little, Brown and Co., 1988.

All That Glitters

Johnson, Donald-Brian and Leslie Pina. *Whiting & Davis Purses: The Perfect Mesh*. Atglen, PA: Schiffer Publishing, 2002.

Lussier, Suzanne. *Art Deco Fashion*. New York: Bullfinch Press, 2003.

Mandelbaum, Howard and Eric Myers. *Screen Deco, a Celebration of High Style in Hollywood*. New York: St. Martin's Press, 1985. Republished: San Francisco: Hennessey & Ingalls, 2001.

Moro, Ginger. *European Designer Jewelry*. Atglen, PA: Schiffer Publishing, 1996.

Raulet, Sylvie. *Art Deco Jewelry*. New York: Rizzoli International, 1985. Republished: London: Thames & Hudson, 2003.

Starr, Steve. *Picture Perfect, Deco Photo Frames 1926–1946*. New York: Rizzoli International, 1991.

NAMES TO NOTE

FURNITURE

Alvar Aalto (Finnish, 1898–1976)
Jacques Adnet (French, 1900–1984)
André Arbus (French, 1903–1969)
Norman Bel Geddes
(American, 1893–1958)
Marcel Breuer (Hungarian/American, 1902–1981)
Pierre Chareau (French, 1883, d. New York, 1950)
Le Corbusier (aka Charles Edouard Jeanneret, Swiss/French, 1887–1965)
Donald Deskey
(American, 1894–1989)
DIM (Décoration Interieur Moderne, 1918–1940s)
Dominique (French firm), founded by André Domin (1883–1962) and Marcel Genevrière (1885–1967)
Michel Dufet (French, 1888–1985)
Maurice Dufrène
(French, 1876–1955)
Jean Dunand (French/Swiss, 1877–1942)
H & L Epstein (British firm, dates unknown, founded by Harry and Lou Epstein)
Paul Follot (French, 1877–1941)
Jean-Michel Frank
(French, 1893–1941)
Paul T. Frankl
(Austrian/American, 1878–1958)
Grand Rapids Chair & Bookcase Co. (American firm, 1911–1956, then merged with Widdicomb)
Eileen Gray (Irish, worked in France, 1878–1976)
André Groult (French, 1884–1966)
Ray Hille (British, dates unknown, active 1920s–1930s)
René Herbst (French, 1891–1982)
Herman Miller (American firm, 1923–present)

Wolfgang Hoffmann (American, 1900–1969)
Howell Manufacturing (American firm, 1930s–1940s)
Paul Iribe (French, 1883–1935)
Léon Jallot (French, 1874–1967)
Betty Joel (British, 1896–1984)
René Joubert (French, d. 1931) and his company Décoration Interieur Moderne (DIM)
Francis Jourdain (French, 1876–1958)
Christian Krass (French, 1868–1957)
Pierre Legrain (French, 1887–1929)
Jules Leleu (French, 1883–1961)
Lloyd Manufacturing (American firm, 1930s–1940s)
Raymond Loewy (French/American, 1893–1986)
La Maitrise (French, boutique in the department store Galeries Lafayette)
Louis Majorelle (French, 1859–1929)
Robert Mallet-Stevens
(French,1886–1945)
Warren McArthur Corporation (American firm); Warren McArthur (1885–1961)
Clément Mère (French, b. 1870)
Ludwig Mies van der Rohe (German/American, 1886–1969)
Jean Pascaud (French, 1903–1966)
Paul Poiret (French, 1879–1944) and Atelier Martine
Pomone (French, boutique in the department store Au Bon Marché)
Alfred Porteneuve (French, Ruhlmann's nephew, dates unknown)
Primavera (French, boutique in the department store Au Printemps)
Eugene Printz (French, 1889–1948)
René Prou (French, 1889–1948)
Armand-Albert Rateau (French, 1882–1937)

Gilbert Rohde (American, 1894–1944)

Royal Metal Furniture Company (American firm, 1930s–1940s)

Jean Royère (French, 1902–1981)

Jacques-Émile Ruhlmann (French, 1879–1933)

Eugene Schoen (American, 1880–1957)

Louis Sognot (French, 1892–1970)

André Sornay (French, 1902–2000)

Simmons Furniture (American firm, 1870–present)

Süe et Mare (French firm, 1919–1928, founded by Louis Süe (1875–1968) and André Mare (1887–1932)

Troy Sunshade Company (American firm, 1887–present)

Walter Dorwin Teague (American, 1883–1960)

Paul Vera (French, 1882–1958)

Karl Emmanuel Martin (Kem) Weber (American, 1889–1963)

Widdicomb Company (American firm, 1865–present)

Frank Lloyd Wright (American, 1867–1959)

Russel Wright (American, 1904–1976)

LAMPS, LIGHTING, AND METALWARE

Oscar B. Bach (American, 1884–1957)

Norman Bel Geddes (American, 1893–1958)

Edgar Brandt (French, 1880–1960)

Albert Cheuret (French, active 1910–1940)

Consolidated Lamp & Glass Company (American firm, 1894–1967)

Daum (French firm, 1878–present)

Degué (French firm, 1920's–1930's)

Donald Deskey (American, 1894–1989)

William Hunt Diederich (Hungarian/American, 1884–1953)

Louis Katona (French, dates unknown)

Paul Kiss (Romanian/French, active 1920s–1930s)

René Lalique (French, 1860–1945)

William Lescaze (American, 1896–1969)

Lightolier (American firm, 1904–present)

Jean Luce (French, 1895–1964)

Majestic Lighting Company (American)

Markel Corporation (American firm, 1930s–1940s)

Muller Frères (French firm, 1895–1933)

Pattyn Products Company (American, active 1930s–1950s)

Jean Perzel (Czechoslovakian/French, b. 1892)

Gilbert Rohde (American, 1894–1944)

John B. Salterini (American, created own firm, 1928–1953)

Charles Schneider (French 1881–1962)

Raymond Subes (French, 1893–1970)

Walter Dorwin Teague (American, 1883–1960)

Walter Von Nessen (German/American, 1889–1943)

Kurt Versen (Swedish/American, 1901–1997)

Russel Wright (American, 1904–1976)

CLOCKS

ATO (French firm, 1922–1948, founded by Léon Hatot)

J. E. Caldwell (American firm, 1839–present)

Paul Frankl (American, 1878–1958)

Albert Guenot (French, 1894–1993)

René Lalique (French, 1860–1945)

Herman Miller (American firm, 1923–present)

Manning Bowman Company (American, 1832–1951)

Pennwood Numechron Company
American firm, 1930s–about 1960)
Jean Puiforcat (French, 1897–1945)
Gilbert Rohde (American, 1894–1944)
Telechron (American firm, 1917–1960, absorbed by GE)
Seth Thomas (American firm, 1813–present)
Karl Emmanuel Martin (Kem)
Weber (American, 1889–1963)

RUGS AND TEXTILES

Ralph Barton (American, 1891–1931)
Donald Deskey (American, 1894–1989)
Marion Dorn (British, 1899–1964)
Helen Dryden (American, 1887–1934)
Raoul Dufy (French, 1877–1953)
Charles Buckles Falls (American, 1874–1960)
John Held, Jr. (American, 1889–1958)
Betty Joel (British, 1896–1984)
Ilonka Karasz (Hungarian/American, 1896–1981)
Edward McKnight Kauffer (American/British, 1890–1954)
Ruth Reeves (American, 1892–1966)
Eliel Saarinen (Finnish/American, 1873–1950)
Bruno da Silva Bruhns (French, active 1915–1935)

DECORATIVE SCULPTURE

Marcel Bouraine (French, active 1918–1935)
Demetre H. Chiparus (Romanian/French, 1888–1950)
Claire Jeanne Roberte Colinet (Belgian, active 1910–1940)
Jean Bernard Descomps (French, 1872–1948)
Pierre Le Faguays (French, b. 1892)

Frankart (American firm, 1921–1932)
Amadeo Gennarelli (Italian/French, active 1915–1930)
Maurice Guiraud–Riviere (French, b. 1881)
Hagenauer (Austrian firm, founded in 1898 by Carl Hagenauer)
Alexander Kelety (Hungarian/French, active 1920–1940)
Joseph Lorenzl (Austrian, active 1915–1930)
Roland Paris (French, b. 1894)
Otto Poertzel (German, 1867–1963)
Ferdinand (Fritz) Preiss (German, 1882–1943)
Bruno Zach (Austrian, active 1918–1935)

FINE ART SCULPTURE

Alexander Archipenko (1887–1964)
Rembrandt Bugatti (Italian, 1884–1916)
Joseph Csaky (Hungarian/French, 1888–1971)
Harriet Whitney Frishmuth (American, 1880–1979)
Malvina Hoffman (American, 1887–1966)
Anna Hyatt Huntington (American, 876–1973)
Carl Paul Jennewein (American, 1890–1978)
Jean Lambert–Rucki (1888–1967)
Lee Lawrie (American, 1877–1963)
Jacques Lipchtyz (French, 1891–1973)
Boris Lovet–Lorski (Lithuanian/French, 1894–1973)
Paul Manship (American, 1885–1966)
Carl Milles (American, 1875–1955)
Gustav Miklos (Hungarian/French, 1888–1967)
Elie Nadelman (American, 1882–1946)
François Pompon (1855–1933)

Edouard Marcel Sandoz (French,
1881–1971)
John Storrs (American, 1885–1956)

SILVER

Charles Boynton (British,
1885–1958)
Cartier (French firm, founded in
1847 by Louis-François Cartier)
Christofle (French firm, founded in
1839 by Joseph-Albert Bouilhet)
Elwood N. Cornell (American, dates
unknown)
La Maison Desny (French firm,
founded by Desnet and René
Nauny)
Jean Desprès (French, worked in the
1930s)
Gorham (American firm,
1831–present)
Jean Goulden (French, 1878–1947)
International Silver Company
(American firm, 1898–present)
Georg Jensen (Danish, 1886–1935)
Ilonka Karasz (Hungarian/Ameri-
can, 1896–1981)
Paul Lobel (American, 1899–1983)
Erik Magnussen (American,
1884–1960)
Peter Muller-Munk (German/Ameri-
can, 1904–1967)
Harald Nielsen (Danish, 1892–1977)
Jean Puiforcat (French, 1897– 1945)
Reed & Barton (American firm,
1824–present)
Louis W. Rice (American, active
1930s)–
Bernard Rice's Sons "Apollo" Silver
Company (American firm, founded
1921)
Eliel Saarinen (Finnish/American,
1873–1950)
William Spratling (American,
worked in Mexico, 1900–1967)
Harold Stabler (British, 1872–1945)
Tetard Frères (French firm, founded
mid–1800s)
Tiffany & Company (American firm,
1837– present)

Walter von Nessen (German/Ameri-
can, 1889–1943)
Karl Emmanuel Martin (Kem)
Weber (American, 1889–1963)
WMF (Württembergische Metallwarenfabrik, German firm,
1880–present)

CHROME

Norman Bel Geddes (American,
1893–1958)
Chase Brass & Copper Company
(American firm, 1876–1976)
Farberware (American firm,
1900–present)
Farber Brothers Krome-Kraft (Amer-
ican firm, 1915–1965)
Lurelle Guild (American,
1898–1985)
Manning Bowman Company
(American firm, 1832–1951)
Rockwell Kent (American,
1882–1971)
Revere Copper and Brass (American
firm, 1801–present)
Ronson Corporation (American
firm, founded in the 1890s by Louis
V. Aronson)
Emile A. Schuelke (American,
1930s, creator of the Penguin cock-
tail shaker)
Walter von Nessen (German/Ameri-
can, 1889–1943)
Russel Wright (American,
1904–1976)
William A. Welden (American,
1892–1970)

GLASS

Gabriel Argy–Rousseau (French,
1885–1953)
Paul D'Avesn (French, worked for
Daum 1920–1933)
Baccarat (French firm, founded
1765)– Especially for perfume
bottles
Cambridge Glass Company (American firm, 1873–1958), especially

from 1930s to 1954 under the owner Wilber L. Orme (American, 1889–1972)

Edouard Cazaux (French, 1889–1974)

Consolidated Lamp & Glass Company (American firm, 1894–1967), especially "Ruba Rombic," 1928, designed by Reuben Haley (American, 1872–1933)

Czech Glass (1920s–1930s, anonymous, mass-produced glass)

Daum (French firm, 1878–present), founded by Antoine Daum (1864–1930) / Auguste Daum (1853–1909)

François-Émile Decorchement (French, 1880–1971)

Degué (French firm, 1920s–1930s)

Etling–La Société Anonyme Edmond Etling–(French firm, 1920s–1930s, did not survive WWII)

André Hunebelle (French firm, produced glass 1920s–1930s)

Lalique (French firm, 1909–present), especially works by

René Lalique (French, 1860–1945)

Marc Lalique (French, 1900–1977)

Legras (French firm, 1864–present)

Libbey Glass Company (American firm, 1878–present), especially works by

    Walter Dorwin Teague (American, 1882–1960)

    Edwin W. Fuerst (American, 1903–1988)

Jean Luce (French, 1895–1964)

Maurice Marinot (French, 1882–1960)

Muller Frères (French, 1895–1936)

Marcel Goupy (French, 1866–?)

Henri Navarre (French, 1885–1971)

Orrefors (Swedish firm, 1898 – present), especially works by

    Simon Gate (1883–1945)

    Edward Hald (1883–1980)

    Vicke Lindstrand (1904–1983)

    Nils Landberg (b. 1907)

Phoenix Glass Company (American firm, acquired by Anchor Hocking in 1970), especially the Sculptured Art Glass line, 1933 to 1958

Sabino (French firm, 1920s–present), founded by Maurius-Ernest Sabino (French, 1878–1961)

George Sakier (American, 1897–1988) especially designs for Fostoria Glass

Cristallerie Schneider (French firm, 1913–1982), founded by Charles Schneider (1881–1962), Especially the line "Le Verre Français" (produced 1918–1939)

Steuben (American firm, 1903–present), especially designs by

    Frederick Carder (1863–1963)

    Walter Dorwin Teague (American, 1882–1960)

    John Monteith Gates (American, active 1930s–1950s)

    Sidney Biehler Waugh (American, 1904–1963)

André Thuret (French, 1898–1965)

Val St. Lambert (Belgian firm, 1825–present)–cut crystal

Verlys (French firm, starting in the 1930s, then also in America until about 1951)

Almaric Walter (French, 1859–1942)

American Mass-Produced Depression Glass

"Cubist" Pattern, 1929–1933—Jeannette Glass

"Manhattan" Pattern, 1938–1939–1943—Anchor Hocking

"Pyramid" Pattern, 1928–1932—Indiana Glass Company

"Tearoom" Pattern, 1926–1931—Indiana Glass Company

CERAMICS

Jacques Adnet (French, 1900–1984)

American Art Clay Company of Indianapolis, or AMACO (American firm)

Augarten (300-year-old Austrian porcelain firm, still producing)

Gabriel Beauvais (French, active 1910–1930)

Boch Frères and Boch Frères Keramis (Belgian firm, 1841–present), especially

works by Boch Art Director Charles Catteau (Belgian, 1880–1966)

René Buthaud (French, 1886–1986)

Carlton Ware (produced by Wiltshaw & Robinson, British firm, 1890–1957)

Edouard Cazaux (French, 1889–1974)

Clarice Cliff (British,1899–1972)

Susie Cooper (British,1902–1995)—Most collectible starting in 1931 with her own firm

Cowan Pottery (American firm, Ohio, 1913–1931), especially designs by:
  Reginald Guy Cowan (1884–1957)
  Alexander Blazys (1894–1963)
  Waylande DeSantis Gregory (1905–1971)
  A. Drexler Jacobson (1895–1972)
  Margaret Postgate (?–1953)
  Viktor Schreckengost (b. 1906)

Émile Decoeur (French, 1876–1953),

Joseph Descompes (French, 1869–1950)

Etling—La Société Anonyme Edmond Etling—(French firm, 1920s–1930s, did not survive WWII)

André Fau (French, active 1920s–1940s)

Frankoma Pottery (1930s–present)

Goldscheider (Austrian firm, 1885–1953)

Gustavsberg (Swedish firm, 1786–present)—especially

Argenta Ware, introduced by chief designer Wilhelm Kage (Swedish, 1889–1960)

Hall China Company (American firm 1903–present), especially "Refrigerator Ware" designed by J. Palin Thorley (British/American, b. 1892)

Homer Laughlin Company (American firm)—especially

Frederick H. Rhead's "Fiesta Ware," originally produced 1936–1972

Raoul Lachenal (French, 1885–1926)

Robert T. Lallemant (French, 1902–1954)

Charles Lemanceau (French, 1905–1980)

Lenci (Italian firm, founded 1919)

Émile Lenoble (French, 1876–1939)

Longwy (French firm, 1789–present)

Jean Mayodon (French, 1893–1967)

Noritake (Japanese firm, founded 1904)

Poole Pottery (Carter, Stabler & Adams, British, founded 1873)

Pomone (French, boutique in the department store Au Bon Marché)

Primavera (French, boutique in the department store Au Printemps)

Charlotte Rhead (British, 1885–1947)

Robj (French firm, 1920–early 1930s)

Rosenthal (German firm, 1870s–present)

Roseville Pottery (American, Ohio, 1898–1954)

Sèvres (French firm, 1750–present), especially works by Robert Bonfils, Émile Decoeur, Jean Dupas, Suzanne Lalique, and Ruhlmann

Shelley (British firm, 1872–1966)

Steubenville Pottery Company (American, Ohio)—especially Russel Wright "American Modern," introduced in 1937

Camille Tharaud (French, 1878–1956)

Villeroy & Boch (German, 1748–present)

Wedgwood (British, 1759 to the present), especially 1930s designs by Keith Murray (British, 1892–1981)

WMF (Württembergische Metallwarenfabrik, German firm, 1880–present)

Vally Wieselthier (Austrian/American, 1895–1945)
Eva Zeisel (Hungarian/American, b. 1906)

FINE PRINTS

James E. Allen (American, 1894–1964)
Alexander Archipenko (Russian–American,1887–1964)
Jolan Gross Bettelheim (Czech/American, 1900–1970)
John Buckland–Wright (British, 1897–1954)
Howard Cook (American, 1901–1980)
Sonia Delaunay (French, 1885–1979)
Raoul Dufy (French, 1877–1953)
Erté (aka Romain de Tirtoff, French, 1892–1990)
Eric Gill (British, 1882–1940)
Louis Icart (French, 1887–1951)
Rockwell Kent (American, 1882–1971)
Jean-Émile Laboureur (French, 1877–1943)
Paul Landacre (American, 1893–1063)
Marie Laurencin (French, 1883–1956)
Clare Leighton (British–American, 1901–1989)
Martin Lewis (American, 1881–1962)
Boris Lovet-Lorski (Lithuanian/French, 1894–1973)
Louis Lozowick (American 1892–1973)
Jan Matulka (American, 1890–1970)
Otis Oldfield (American, 1890–1969)
William S. Schwartz (Russian/American, 1896–1933)
Benton Spruance (American, 1904–1962)
Harry Sternberg (American, 1904–2002)

Charles Turzak (American, 1899–1985)
Lynd Ward (American)

POSTERS

Otto Anton (German, 1895–1976)
Otto Baumberger (Swiss, 1889–1961)
Lucian Bernhard (German, 1883–1972)
Joseph Binder (Austrian/American, 1898–1972)
Robert Bonfils (French, 1886–1972)
Roger Broders (French, 1883–1953)
Leonetto Cappiello (Italian, worked in France, 1875–1942)
Émile Cardinaux (Swiss, 1877–1936)
Jean Carlu (French, 1900–1997)
A. M. Cassandre (aka Adolphe Mouron, French, 1901–1968)
Jean Chassaing (French, 1905–1938)
Paul Colin (French, 1892–1986)
Pierre Commarmond (French, 1897–1983)
Austin Cooper (British/Canadian, 1890–1964)
Jean-Gabriel Domergue (French, 1889–1962)
Marcello Dudovich (Italian, 1878–1962)
Maurice Dufrène (French, 1876–1955)
Jean Dupas (French, 1882–1964)
Leon Dupin (French, 1898–1971)
Robert Falcucci (French, 1900–1989)
Pierre Fix-Masseau (French, 1905–1994)
Charles Gesmar (French, 1900–1928)
William H. Gispen (Dutch, 1890–1981)
Werner Graul (German, 1905–1984)
Ludwig Hohlwein (German, 1874–1949)
Edward McKnight Kauffer (American/British, 1890–1954)

Gustave Krollman (American, b. 1888)
Julien Lacaze (French, 1886–1971)
Franz Lenhart (German, worked in Italy, 1898–1992)
Georges Lepape (French, 1887–1971)
Joseph Leyendecker (American, 1874–1951)
Maurice Logan (American, 1886–1977)
Charles Loupot (French, 1892–1962)
Leo Marfurt (Belgian, 1894–1977)
Sascha Maurer (American, 1897–1961)
Herbert Matter (Swiss, 1907–1984)
Leopoldo Metlicovitz (Italian, 1868–1944)
Frank Newbould (British, 1887–1950)
Marcello Nizzoli (Italian, 1887–1960)
Tom Purvis (British, 1888–1959)
Leslie Ragan (American, 1897–1972)
Walter Schnackenberg (German, 1880–1961)
Sepo (aka Severo Pozzati, Italian, 1895–1983)
Albert Solon (French, 1897–1973)
Johann von Stein (Dutch, 1896–1965)
Fred Taylor (British, 1875–1963)
Adolph Treidler (American, 1886–1981)
William Welsh (American, 1889–?)
Jupp Wiertz (German, 1881–1939)
Jan Wijga (Dutch, 1902–1978)
Pierre Zenobel (French, 1905–1996)

FASHION ILLUSTRATIONS & POCHOIRS

Paul Allier (French, 1883–1967)
George Barbier (French, 1882–1932)
Edouard Benedictus (French, 1878–1932)
Edouardo Benito (Spanish, 1891–?)

Umberto Brunelleschi (Italian, 1879–1949)
Georges Lepape (French, 1887–1971)
Charles Martin (French, 1884–1934)
André Marty (French, 1882–1974)
François-Louis Schmied (1873–1941)
E. A. Seguy (French, active 1915–1930)
Georges Valmier (French, 1885–1937)

MAGAZINE COVERS

Asia Magazine (1924–1933)
Frank McIntosh (American, b. 1901)
Fortune Magazine (started 1929)
Ernest Hamlin Baker (American, 1889–1975)
Joseph Binder (Austrian/American, 1898–1972)
A.M. Cassandre (French, 1901–1968)
Covers by Miguel Covarrubias (1904–1957)
Covers by Paolo Garetto (Italian, 1903–1989)
Covers by Fernand Léger (French, 1881–1955)
Covers by Antonio Petrucelli (American, b. 1907)
Diego Rivera (Mexican, 1886–1957)
Charles Sheeler (American, 1883–1965)
Fernand Léger (French, 1881–1955)
Herbert Bayer (American, 1900–1985)
Harper's Bazaar (covers from 1915–1930s)
Erté (aka Romain de Tirtoff, French, 1892–1990)
A.M. Cassandre (French, 1901–1968)
Vanity Fair (covers from 1913–1930s)
Eduardo Benito (Spanish, b. 1891)
George Bolin (American, dates unknown)

Miguel Covarrubias (Mexican, 1904–1957)
Paolo Garetto (Italian, 1903–1989)
Georges Lepape (French, 1887–1971)
Vogue (covers from 1913–1930s)
Georges Lepape (French, 1887–1971)
George W. Plank (American, 1883–1965)
Woman's Home Companion (covers from 1920s– 1930s)
William Welsh (American, 1889–?)

INDUSTRIAL DESIGN

Egmont Arens (American, 1888–1966)
Norman Bel Geddes (American, 1893–1958)
Donald Deskey (American, 1894–1989)

Henry Dreyfuss (American, 1904–1972)
Raymond Loewy (French/American, 1893–1986)
Manning Bowman Company (American, 1832–1951)
Polaroid Corporation (American firm, founded 1937, declared bankruptcy 2001)
Gilbert Rohde (American, 1894–1944)
Viktor Schreckengost (b. 1906)
Walter Dorwin Teague (American, 1883–1960)
John Vassos (American, 1898–1985)
Westinghouse Electric Company (American firm, founded 1886)
Karl Emmanuel Martin (Kem) Weber (American, 1889–1963)
Russel Wright (American, 1904–1976)

INDEX

ABOUT THE
AUTHOR

Tony Fusco.
Photo by Robert
Four.

Tony Fusco is Founder and President of the Art Deco Society of Boston (ADSB), and served as Facilitator for the International Coalition of Art Deco Societies (ICADS) from 1992 to 1999. He is the author of *The Official Identification and Price Guide to Art Deco* (1988, 1993), and *The Official Identification and Price Guide to Posters* (1990, 1994). His byline has appeared in more than fifty magazines and periodicals.

Since 1979, Fusco & Four has provided marketing and public relations services to more than 300 arts and leisure businesses and non-profit arts organizations. Along with his partner, Robert Four, a photographer and the agency's Art Director, he produces the Boston International Fine Art Show and has served as consultant to Miami Modernism and other 20th-century design clients. In 1989 Fusco & Four also founded Twentieth Century Works Of Art, a fine art dealership that specializes in American and European works of art from 1900 to 1950. Fusco & Four provides consulting and appraisal services in Art Deco, 20th-century design and vintage posters. For more information, by appointment only, call or write: Fusco & Four, 1 Murdock Terrace, Boston, MA 02135. (617) 787-2637, or visit www.ArtDecoNetwork.com.